Barbados

Sarah Cameron

Credits

Footprint credits

Editor: Stephanie Rebello
Production and layout: Emma Bryers
Maps and cover: Kevin Feeney

Publisher: Patrick Dawson
Managing Editor: Felicity Laughton
Advertising: Elizabeth Taylor
Sales and marketing: Kirsty Holmes

Photography credits

Front cover: Jdazuelos/Dreamstime.com
Back cover: Shutterstock/P.HB.sz
(Richard Semik)

Printed in Great Britain by 4edge Limited,
Hockley, Essex

MIX
Paper from
responsible sources
FSC™ C020822
www.fsc.org

Every effort has been made to ensure that
the facts in this guidebook are accurate.
However, travellers should still obtain advice
from consulates, airlines, etc, about travel
and visa requirements before travelling.
The authors and publishers cannot accept
responsibility for any loss, injury or
inconvenience however caused.

Publishing information

Footprint *Focus Barbados*
1st edition
© Footprint Handbooks Ltd
October 2013

ISBN: 978 1 909268 32 6
CIP DATA: A catalogue record for this book
is available from the British Library

® Footprint Handbooks and the Footprint
mark are a registered trademark of
Footprint Handbooks Ltd

Published by Footprint
6 Riverside Court
Lower Bristol Road
Bath BA2 3DZ, UK
T +44 (0)1225 469141
F +44 (0)1225 469461
footprinttravelguides.com

Distributed in the USA by Globe Pequot
Press, Guilford, Connecticut

The content of Footprint *Focus Barbados*
is based on Footprint's *Caribbean Islands
Handbook*, which was researched and
written by Sarah Cameron.

Contents

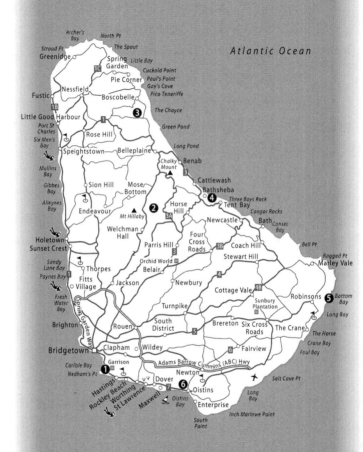

Atlantic Ocean

Archer's Bay
North Pt
The Spout
Stroud Pt
Greenidge
Spring Garden
Little Bay
Cuckold Point
Pie Corner
Paul's Point
Gay's Cove
Pico Tenariffe
Nessfield
Boscobelle
The Choyce
Fustic
Little Good Harbour
Green Pond
Port St Charles
Rose Hill
Six Men's Bay
Speightstown
Belleplaine
Long Pond
Mullins Bay
Sion Hill
Mose Bottom
Chalky Mount
Benab
Cattlewash
Bathsheba
Gibbes Bay
Alleynes Bay
Endeavour
Mt Hillaby
Horse Hill
Three Bays Rock
Tent Bay
Congor Rocks
Holetown
Sunset Crest
Welchman Hall
Newcastle
Bath
Conset Bay
Sandy Lane Bay
Thorpes
Parris Hill
Four Cross Roads
Coach Hill
Bell Pt
Paynes Bay
Fitts Village
Orchid World
Belair
Stewart Hill
Ragged Pt
Marley Vale
Fresh Water Bay
Jackson
Newbury
Cottage Vale
Robinsons
Bottom Bay
Brighton
Rouen
Turnpike
Sunbury Plantation
Long Bay
Bridgetown
Clapham
Wildey
South District
Brereton
Six Cross Roads
The Crane
The Horse
Crane Bay
Foul Bay
Carlisle Bay
Garrison
Adams Barrow Cummins (ABC) Hwy
Fairview
Nedham's Pt
Newton
Salt Cave Pt
Hastings
Rockley Beach
Worthing
St Lawrence
Dover
Maxwell
Oistins Bay
Oistins
Enterprise
Long Bay
Inch Marlowe Point
South Point

N

2 km
2 miles

Tourism and Barbados go together like rum and coke, flying fish and chips. Visitors come back time and again to tune in to the rhythm and lime with a Banks beer. You can pay thousands of dollars to be truly cosseted along with music moguls and supermodels, or you can cater for yourself and go shopping with Bajans. The west coast is the place to be seen, commonly referred to as the Platinum Coast. The south is for beach life, night life, fun and games, the package holiday end of the market with a cheerful, relaxed atmosphere and the best sand. The east is wild and untamed, a world apart, where the Atlantic crashes into cliffs, eroding the coastline and creating beaches of a rare beauty. Head to the hills inland to explore relics of colonial days such as plantation houses, signal towers, tropical gardens, museums and rum distilleries.

Of all the islands in the eastern Caribbean, Barbados is unique in that it remained British throughout its colonial history, without being passed from one European master to another. The island is divided into 11 parishes named after 10 saints, Christ Church being the 11th. Many parish churches are impressive buildings. Towns have the charming English seaside resort names of Hastings, Brighton or Dover and it was often referred to as Little England in the past, not always as a compliment. Since independence in 1966 the country has tried to shake off that white middle-class suburban image and has moved closer in cultural terms to North America while also pursuing its African roots. Drum music, banned by colonial masters to prevent the organization of slave rebellions, and 'tuk' bands are an essential part of carnival processions. Calypso, soca and pan music blast from vehicles, as well as being the centre piece of Crop Over, the boisterous festival celebrating the end of the sugar harvest. However, some habits die hard. You can still go to a polo match and be offered tea and cucumber sandwiches, or watch Sunday cricket on the village green. A Test Match at the Kensington Oval, though, is a sight to behold – an example of how an English sport has been turned into pure Afro-Caribbean pageantry.

Planning your trip

Best time to visit Barbados

Any time of year is holiday time in Barbados but some months are better than others, depending on what you want to do. The climate is tropical, but rarely excessively hot because of the trade winds. Temperatures vary between 21°C and 35°C, the coolest and driest time being December-May, and a wet and hotter season June-November. Rain is usually heavy when it comes but Barbados has rarely been hit by hurricanes. When Tropical Storm Lily struck in September 2002, around 150 houses were damaged, mostly in the Parish of St Philip, but there was no loss of life. Bajans said they hadn't seen anything like it since Hurricane Janet in 1955.

If you want to join in a carnival atmosphere then time your visit for **Crop Over** in July-August, but book flights, accommodation and car hire in plenty of time as everything is very busy. Bajans return home from all over the world for **Crop Over** and the partying goes on for five weeks. Other musical events worth aiming for are the **Jazz Festival** in January, **Holders Season** in March and the **Celtic Festival** in May with lots of music, dance and sports. Cricket lovers should aim to take in a **Test Match** or the **BUSTA Cup** to see top international players at the Kensington Oval, but there are cricket festivals at other times of the year and of course matches every Sunday in villages around the island. Even if you know nothing about cricket a match at the Oval is worth seeing for the audience. The stands throb to the beat of drums and whistles, calypso and comedy. This is more than just the national sport, it's almost a religion.

Getting to Barbados

Air

Barbados' popularity as a tourist destination has resulted in good transport connections with many flights from Europe and North and South America. The **Grantley Adams International Airport** ① *www.gaia.bb*, is 16 km from Bridgetown, near the resorts on the south coast and connected to the west coast beaches by the ABC Highway which bypasses the capital. Flights to Barbados are heavily booked at Christmas and for Crop Over (July-early August).

Flights from the UK The main scheduled carriers from the UK are **British Airways** and **Virgin Atlantic** from London Gatwick, while there are flights from several cities with **flythomascook** (via Antigua or St Lucia), **Monarch** and **Thomson Flights** and connections for scheduled flights with **Flybe**, **Caribbean Airlines** flies from Gatwick to Barbados via Trinidad.

Flights from the rest of Europe Condor flies from Frankfurt via Tobago but most flights from European cities connect through London with **British Airways**. Other connecting flights are available with **Air Canada** and **American Airlines** if you want to go via North America.

Flights from North America Air Canada, American Airlines, Delta, Jet Blue, US Airways, Canjet and West Jet as well as several charter services fly from cities across

Don't miss...

1 **The Garrison**, page 29.
2 **Flower Forest**, page 42.
3 **St Nicholas Abbey**, page 48.
4 **Bathsheba**, page 52.
5 **Bottom Bay**, page 57.
6 **Oistins Friday Fish Fry**, page 60.

Numbers relate to the map on page 4.

the USA and Canada. **Caribbean Airlines** has connecting flights from New York, Florida and Toronto via Jamaica and Trinidad.

Flights from Australia and New Zealand There are no direct flights and connections must be made through North America or London.

Flights from the Caribbean LIAT has lots of direct flights from Antigua, Dominica, St Lucia, St Vincent, Grenada, Trinidad and Guyana, while at their Antigua hub they connect to the Dominican Republic, Puerto Rico, St Thomas, St Croix, Tortola, Anguilla, Sint Maarten, St Kitts, Nevis and Guadeloupe, and from Trinidad you can fly on to Curaçao. **Caribbean Airlines** connects Barbados to its hubs in Trinidad and in Jamaica, from where they connect to other islands: Sint Maarten, Antigua, St Lucia, Grenada, Tobago and Nassau, as well as to Guyana, Suriname and Caracas. Charter service is available with **Executive Air** to and from St Vincent and the Grenadines, Trinidad and Tobago, Grand Cayman and Cuba, as well as to Canada and Florida. They also operate an **Air Ambulance** service. Other airlines operating charter flights, day tours and air taxi services are **Trans Island Air**, **St Vincent and Grenadines Air** and **Mustique Airways**. GOL flies from Brazil with other South American connections.

Airport information The airport is modern and well equipped. There are two linked terminals, one for departures and one for arrivals. There is a helpful **Tourism Authority office**, **Barbados National Bank**, car hire agencies (**Courtesy Rent-ACar**, **Drive-a-matic** and **Stoute's Car Rental**) in the public area to the left as you exit the arrivals terminal, and quite a wide range of shops including **Cave Sheperd**, an inbound duty-free shop (very useful, saves carrying heavy bottles on the plane).

Taxis stop just outside customs. Check the notice board on the left as you come out of arrivals, as it gives the official taxi fares. Alternatively see www.gaia.bb/content/taxi-rates-airport. Authorized taxis have a yellow sticker on the side, The taxi dispatcher will give you a trip form and advice on fares. Drivers may attempt to charge more if you haven't checked. There is a bus stop on the main road just across the car park, with buses running hourly along the south coast to Bridgetown, or (over the road) to the **Crane**. Across the car park there are two lively rum shops; the shop in the gas station is open when terminal shops are closed, selling food, papers, etc. Next to the departures terminal is a Concorde museum housing the ex-British Airways plane G-BOAE. Very few flights arrive late at night, but if you are delayed, there are hotels a short taxi ride from the airport, see Where to stay, page 64 (South Coast).

Sea

Cruise ships call at Bridgetown and some passengers choose to start or break their journey here, but otherwise there is no passenger shipping. The cruise ship terminal, just north of Bridgetown, has shops, restaurants, communications centre, tourist information, tour operators, taxis and a chattel house craft village.

Transport in Barbados

Road

The island is fairly small but it can take a surprisingly long time to travel as the rural roads are narrow and winding. Although the island is only 34 km long and 22 km wide, there are about 1475 km of paved roads and plenty of ways to get lost. The Adams Barrow Cummins highway runs from the airport to a point between Brighton and Prospect, north of Bridgetown. This road skirts the east edge of the capital, giving access by various roads into the city and to the west and east coasts. Its roundabouts are named after eminent Bajans, including Sir Garfield Sobers, Errol Barrow and Everton Weekes. North of Bridgetown, heading up the west coast, is Highway 1, giving access to all the beach hotels. Highway 2A runs parallel inland, going through the sugar cane fields and allowing rather speedier access to the north of the island. The highway and roads into Bridgetown get jammed morning and afternoon; the city centre is worst in the middle of the day. Minibuses and route taxis run around the capital, cheaply and efficiently, but are terribly slow in rush hour.

Bus

Buses are cheap, frequent and crowded. Flat fare of B$2 per journey anywhere on the island, so if you change buses you pay again. The drivers do not have change on the public buses so exact fare is required and no foreign coins are accepted. If you are boarding at a terminal, however, you can get change from the cashier, open 0700-2200. Almost all the routes radiate in and out of Bridgetown, so cross-country journeys are time-consuming if you are staying outside the city centre. However, travelling by bus can be fun. There are some circuits which work quite well; for example: 1) any south coast bus to Oistins, then cross country College Savannah bus to the east coast, then direct bus back to Bridgetown; 2) any west coast bus to Speightstown, then bus back to Bathsheba on the east coast, then direct bus back to Bridgetown. Out of town bus stops are marked simply 'To City' or 'Out of City'. For the south coast ask for **Silver Sands** route.

Around Bridgetown, there are plenty of small yellow privately owned minibuses with B licence plates and route taxis with ZR licence plates; elsewhere, the big blue and yellow buses (exact fare required or tokens sold at the bus terminal) belong to the Transport Board, www.transportboard.com. Private buses tend to stick to urban areas while the public buses run half empty in rural areas and in the evening. There is a City Circle route, clockwise and anti-clockwise round the inner suburbs of Bridgetown which starts in Lower Green.

Terminals for the south: Fairchild Street for public buses, clean, modern; Probyn Street, or just across Constitution River from Fairchild Street for minibuses; further east by Constitution River for ZR vans. Terminals for the west: Lower Green for public buses; west of Post Office for minibuses; Princess Alice Highway for ZR vans, but from 1800-2400 all leave from Lower Green. During the rush hour, all these terminals are chaotic, particularly during school term. On most routes, the last bus leaves at, or soon after, midnight and the first bus leaves at 0500. There is also a terminal in Speightstown and a sub-terminal in Oistins.

There are two routes from the airport: Yorkshire buses go straight to Bridgetown, others go along the south coast past the hotels to Bridgetown. For a shopping trip into Bridgetown from the south or west coast hotels from Monday to Saturday, call the **Bridgetown Visitor Shuttle** ① *T431 2078, US$3, 0830-1600*. It is of course cheaper to hop on a regular bus for B$2.

The **Transport Board** also runs Sunday scenic bus tours starting at 1400 from Independence Square, B$20 adults, B$12 children. On the first Sunday of the month they go to Speightstown, Farley Hill, East Coast Road; on the second Sunday to Cherry Tree Hill, Little Bay, River Bay; on the third Sunday to Foul Bay, Three Houses Park, Bath; and on the fourth Sunday to Bathsheba, St. John's Church, King George V Park, Silver Sands. Tickets are available from the change booths at Fairchild Street or Princess Alice Terminals and the **Transport Board Headquarters** ① *T310 3568*.

Car

Drive on the left. Drivers need a US$5 visitor's driving permit (Visitor Registration Certificate), valid for two months, even if you have an International Driving Licence. Car hire companies will usually sort it out for you. Drivers must be over 21 and under 80 and have held a licence for a minimum of two years. Car hire is efficient and generally reliable. Mini mokes, jeeps, vans and air conditioned cars are all available. A medium-sized car or a mini moke will cost on average US$90-100 a day, US$400 a week, but you can get cheaper deals with small companies. There are often discounts available (including free driver's permit) and tourist magazines frequently contain 10% discount vouchers. There are some 60 car rental companies on the island, of which only three have offices at the airport. Fuel prices rise in line with international prices. The speed limit is 80, 60, or 40 kph depending on the type of road. Tourist maps are notoriously short on detail as navigational tools. John Mann's BajanNav, http://bajannav.com/, has been recommended as an alternative to getting lost, either in the city or in the countryside and is highly accurate. Many rental companies offer gps systems as well as child booster seats for an extra fee. All charges for car hire, excess waiver and other extras are subject to VAT of 17.5%. Gasoline costs about US$2.50 per litre.

Cycling

Bridgetown is not recommended for cyclists. The roads are dangerously busy, traffic moves quite fast round the one way system and the road surface is uneven and potholed. Out of town you should be careful on narrow, twisting roads, which also have potholes. There have been many accidents with bicycles and many people who rent bikes lose their deposit because of damage or theft, so it can work out expensive. Besides being dangerous and expensive it is also hot work. Take lots of water and sun screen.

Taxi

There are plenty of taxis at the airport, main hotels, and in Bridgetown. There are standard fares, displayed just outside 'arrivals' at the airport, and are also listed in the *Visitor* and the *Sunseeker*. From the airport to St Lawrence Gap is US$15.50, to Bridgetown US$23, to Holetown US$29, to Speightstown US$36.50. Taxi fares start from the basic tariff of US$8 and if they have to wait for you there is a US$7.50 charge per hour of waiting time. You may have to bargain hard for tours by taxi but always agree a fare in advance.

Walking

The sights of central Bridgetown can be toured on foot in a morning with no difficulty. The Tourism Authority does a useful free leaflet with map for a self-guided walking tour of Bridgetown. There is a good walking route along the old east coast railway track, from Bath to Bathsheba and on to Cattlewash. For organized hiking tours, see page 75.

Where to stay in Barbados

Tourism is the major industry on Barbados and there is a wide selection of hotels, guesthouses, apartments and villas, providing some 10,000 registered and unregistered guest rooms. Barbados is not for the impecunious, it is an upmarket destination. Visitors come here for a treat and expect – and receive – excellent service and value for money. Unusually for the Caribbean, most of the hotels are independently run. Generally, the top hotels in the super luxury category, costing well over US$300 a night, are on the west coast. Places such as **Sandy Lane** are among the world's top resorts, where you can get every conceivable service and luxury. Small and chic hotels are also to be found here. Cheap and cheerful places can be found on the south coast, but many of these are concrete block, characterless hotels usually booked as package holidays. All-inclusives are to be avoided as the food quickly becomes boring and you will miss out on the fun of selecting from the huge choice of places to eat. The best 'getaways' are on the east coast at Bathsheba, where the landscape is rugged and breezy, air conditioning is rarely needed and the atmosphere is completely different. If you are a night owl, this is not the place for you as there is little entertainment and people tend to go to bed early, having had an active day.

Self-catering is popular on Barbados, partly because restaurants are not cheap, and if there is a group of you, you can find good value places to stay. Despite the reputation of the west coast as expensive – it is nicknamed the 'platinum coast' – you can find an apartment to rent for as little as US$25 a night per person if you are not too demanding and don't mind walking a few minutes to the beach. Try **Owners Direct** ⓘ www.ownersdirect.co.uk, for a wide range of properties to rent. To get a really Bajan feel, look out for renovated chattel houses for rent, these are popular and are charming places to stay for a couple or small group. A two-bedroomed chattel house rents for around US$75-125 a night, depending on the season, length of stay and proximity to the sea. The décor may not have that 'interior designer' look, but will be of a good standard with all the amenities and equipment you need. Guesthouses are another budget option, some of which are like small hotels but others are more in the line of bed and breakfast in a family house. If meals are available, you can rely on being able to sample local ingredients and recipes. The Barbados Tourism Authority lists a range of hotels, guesthouses and apartments around the island. For small, low-priced hotels try www.intimatehotelsbarbados.com and www.shoestringbarbados.com.

Food and drink in Barbados

Just as Bajan culture is a blend of British and African traditions, so the cuisine of Barbados is a mix of British and West African tastes and ingredients, developed over the centuries with some other flavours brought to the pot by immigrants from other nations such as India. The need for carbohydrates to fuel slave labour and arduous work in the sugar cane fields has led to a diet based on starchy vegetables known as ground provisions, while difficulties in storing meat and fish in the tropical heat led to common use of salt meat

Price codes

Where to stay

$$$$ over US$150   **$$$** US$66-150
$$ US$30-65   **$** under US$30
Price of a double room in high season, including taxes.

Restaurants

$$$ over US$12   **$$** US$7-12   **$** US$6 and under
Prices for a two-course meal for one person, excluding drinks or service charge.

and fish, pickles and other preserves. Sugar, the main crop of the island for generations, features heavily in both food and drink, reaching perfection in the production of rum.

Food

Fresh fish is excellent and sold at the markets in Oistins, Bridgetown and elsewhere in the late afternoon and evening, when the fishermen come in with their catch. It is a fascinating sight to watch the speed and skill with which women fillet flying fish and bag them up for sale. The main fish season is December-May, when there is less risk of stormy weather at sea. Flying fish are the national emblem and a speciality with two or three fillets to a plate, eaten with chips, breaded in a sandwich (flying fish cutter) or with an elegant sauce. Dolphin fish, also called Dorado or Mahi Mahi on restaurant menus, and kingfish are larger steak-fish. Snapper is excellent. Sea eggs are the roe of the white sea urchin, and are delicious but not often available as they are increasingly rare and in need of protection. There is also plenty of local crab, lobster, conch, octopus and shrimp/prawns.

Cou-cou is a filling starchy dish made from breadfruit or corn meal with okra, peppers and hot sauce. Jug-jug is a Christmas speciality made from guinea corn, pigeon peas and salt meat, supposedly descended from the haggis of the poor white Scottish settlers exiled to the island after the failed Monmouth Rebellion of 1685. Pudding and souse is a huge dish of pickled breadfruit, black pudding and pork. Conkie is a corn-based dish often referred to as stew dumpling, traditionally made and sold during November, originally to celebrate the failure of Guy Fawkes' attempt to blow up the Houses of Parliament and King James I, and later to celebrate Independence from British colonial rule. Conkie contains spices, sugar, pumpkin, corn meal, coconut and sometimes raisins or cherries, all wrapped and steamed in a banana leaf, served hot.

There is a riot of tropical fruit and vegetables: unusual and often unidentifiable objects as well as more familiar items found in supermarkets in Europe and North America but with ten times the flavour. The best bananas in the world are grown in the Caribbean on small farms using the minimum of chemicals, if not organic. They are cheap and incredibly sweet and unlike anything you can buy at home. Many of the wonderful tropical fruits you will come across in juices or in ice cream. Don't miss the rich flavours of the soursop, the guava or the sapodilla. Mangoes in season drip off the trees and those that don't end up on your breakfast plate can be found squashed in abundance all over the roads. Caribbean oranges are often green when ripe, as there is no cold season to bring out the orange colour, and are meant for juicing not peeling. Portugals are like tangerines and easy to peel. The grapefruit originated in Barbados in the 18th century, crossing a sweet orange and a bitter citrus called a shaddock, brought from Polynesia by Captain

Shaddock. Avocados are nearly always sold unripe, so wait several days before attempting to eat them. Avocado trees also provide a surplus of fruit and you will be doing everyone a favour if you eat as many as possible. Avocados have been around since the days of the Arawaks, who also cultivated cassava and cocoa, but many vegetables have their origins in the slave trade, brought over to provide a starchy diet for the slaves. The breadfruit, a common staple rich in carbohydrates and vitamins A, B and C, was brought from the South Seas in 1793 by Captain Bligh, perhaps more famous for the mutiny on the *Bounty*. It is eaten in a variety of ways in Barbados: with tomato and onion, a cucumber and lime souse, mashed like a potato or as wafer-thin crisps. It is one of the many forms of starch popular in local cooking, others include sweet potato, yam, eddo, green banana, plantain, bakes, cassava, rice, pasta and potato. Rice usually comes mixed with pigeon peas, black eye peas or split peas. Macaroni cheese is a popular accompaniment, referred to as 'pie'.

With sugar being grown on the island, Bajans have developed a sweet tooth. It is worth trying tamarind balls, guava cheese, chocolate fudge and peanut brittle, while for dessert, coconut bread, Bajan baked custard and lemon meringue pie are firm favourites.

Drink

There are hundreds of different rums in the Caribbean, each island producing the best, of course. Barbados is one of the main producers and you can find some excellent brands: Mount Gay, Cockspur, Malibu, Foursquare and St Nicholas Abbey. Generally the younger, light rums are used in cocktails and aged, dark rums are drunk on the rocks or treated as you might a single malt whisky. Barbados rum is probably the best in the English-speaking Caribbean, unless of course you come from Jamaica, or Guyana or … It is worth paying a bit extra for a good brand such as VSOP or Old Gold, or for the slightly sweeter Sugar Cane Brandy, unless you are going to drink it with Coca Cola, in which case anything will do. A rum and cream liqueur, *Crisma*, is popular in cocktails or on the rocks. Mount Gay produce a vanilla and a mango flavoured rum. *Falernum* is sweet, sometimes slightly alcoholic, with a hint of vanilla and great in a rum cocktail instead of sugar syrup. *Corn and oil* is rum and falernum. *Mauby* is bitter, made from tree bark and non-alcoholic. It is watered down like a fruit squash and can be refreshing with lots of ice. *Sorrel* is a bright red Christmas drink made with hibiscus sepals and spices; it is very good with white rum. Banks beer has Bajan Light and other beers. Water is of excellent quality, it comes mostly from deep wells sunk into the coral limestone, but there is bottled water if you prefer.

Eating out

There are a number of excellent restaurants on Barbados, with several of gourmet standard. Some of these are in the luxury hotels such as **Sandy Lane**, but you don't have to go to a hotel for cordon bleu cuisine. Many of the chefs have been around a bit, working in high class kitchens in London or Paris before trying a spell in the Caribbean, bringing a variety of skills to the task of preparing tropical ingredients. Eating out is not cheap, and restaurants will charge around US$12-40 for a main course, but standards are high and the settings often special; you may get an open air waterfront table or a garden terrace, maybe even a table on the beach. The majority of places to eat are clustered around Holetown on the west coast and St Lawrence Gap on the south coast, where there is a wide variety, allowing you to indulge in Italian, Mexican, Indian, French, Japanese or whatever takes your fancy. In Bridgetown there are several cheap, canteens for office workers where you can get a filling lunch for around US$6, and around the island there are beach bars for lunch, but what is lacking are Bajan restaurants serving cheap, local food in the evenings. A few rum

Rum cocktails

There is nothing better at the end of a busy day than finding a spot overlooking the sea with a rum in your hand to watch the sunset and look out for the green flash. The theory is that the more rum you drink, the more likely you are to see this flash of green on the horizon as the sun goes down.

There are hundreds of different rums in the Caribbean, each island producing the best, of course. Barbados is one of the main producers and you can find some excellent brands. Generally, the younger, light rums are used in cocktails and aged, dark rums are drunk on the rocks or treated as you might a single malt whisky. Cocktails first became popular after the development of ice-making in the USA in 1870, but boomed in the 1920s partly because of prohibition in the USA and the influx of visitors to Cuba, the Bahamas and other islands, escaping stringent regulations. People have been drowning their rum in cola ever since the Americans brought bottled drinks in to Cuba during the war against Spain at the end of the 19th century, hence the name, **Cuba Libre**. You can in fact adapt any cocktail recipe to substitute other spirits and incorporate rum. It makes an excellent **Bloody Mary**, the spicier the better.

One of the nicest and most refreshing cocktails is a **Daiquirí**, invented in Santiago de Cuba in 1898 by an engineer in the Daiquirí mines. The natural version combines 1½ tablespoons of sugar, the juice of half a lime, some drops of maraschino liqueur, 1½ oz light dry rum and a lot of shaved ice, all mixed in a blender and then served piled high in a wide, chilled champagne glass with a straw. You can also have fruit versions, with strawberry, banana, peach or pineapple, using fruit or fruit liqueur.

Everybody has heard of the old favourite, **Piña Colada**, which can be found on all the islands and is probably the most popular of the fruit-based cocktails, ideal by the side of the pool. Combine and blend coconut liqueur, pineapple juice, light dry rum and shaved ice, then serve with a straw in a glass, a pineapple or a coconut.

Many hotels offer you a welcome cocktail when you stagger out of the taxi, jet-lagged from your transatlantic flight. This is often an over-sweet, watered-down punch, with a poor quality rum and sickly fruit juice. You are more likely to find something palatable in the bar, but it always depends on which blend of juice the barman favours. The standard recipe for a **rum punch** is: 'one of sour, two of sweet, three of strong and four of weak'. If you measure that in fluid ounces, it comes out as 1 oz of lime juice, 2 oz of syrup (equal amounts of sugar and water, boiled for a few minutes), 3 oz of rum and 4 oz of water, fruit juices, ginger ale, or whatever takes your fancy. You could add ice and a dash of Angostura Bitters from Trinidad, use nutmeg syrup from Grenada or Falernum from Barbados instead of sugar syrup, and garnish it with a slice of lime. Delicious.

shops sell fried chicken and there are some fast food places, but nothing else at the budget end of the scale after dark. Oistins on a Friday night is a major event for both Bajans and tourists. Lots of small shops sell fish meals and other food, dub music one end and at the other a small club where they play oldies for ballroom dancing. It continues on Saturday and Sunday, though a bit quieter, and some food places also stay open through the week.

There is something going on nearly every month in Barbados: carnival celebrations, sporting fixtures, music and cultural festivals, something for everyone. The main carnival is Crop Over, which celebrates the end of the sugar cane harvest. For about 30 years it went uncelebrated because of the Second World War and subsequent economic difficulties, but was resurrected for tourist purposes in 1974. Since then it has grown into a major celebration of Bajan culture enjoyed by all and nobody gets much work done during the 5 weeks that it lasts: 'more than a carnival, sweet fuh days'. Many villages will also hold a 'street fair' from time to time. For a diary of events and festivals see http://barbados.org/eventcd.htm.

January

Barbados Horticultural Society (BHS) Annual Flower Show Held over the last weekend at BHS Headquarters, Balls, Christ Church, T428 5889, www.horticulture barbados.com. The BHS counts some very experienced horticulturists among its members and has been exhibiting at the RHS' Chelsea Flower Show annually since 1988, winning numerous medals.

February

Holetown Festival www.holetownfestival barbados.org. The festival commemorates the first settlers' landing St James in Feb1627. There are parades with floats during the day, all well organized and restrained, nothing outrageous. The Mallalieu Motor Collection lends its vintage cars, one of which carries Miss Holetown; a military band parades behind 3 police horses, a few kids march in costume, there are 1 or 2 masked performers, but the event is hugely popular with crowds lining the street from Sunset Crest to the Post Office. Along the grass verge, stalls are set up, selling jewelry, food, T-shirts, wraps, toys, tat, art, and of course the ubiquitous rumshops and Banks

beer. All do good business with tourists and locals alike. In the evening there are different events on offer. Don't miss the police band playing on stage at the edge of the beach. This is Little England par excellence. The audience sits on neat rows of chairs on the sand, politely listening, a very colonial image against the setting sun, until the band tries to sell its latest CD. There are other, more contemporary shows on different nights, but none goes on beyond 2200.

March

Holders Season (22 Mar-5 Apr 2014) T432 6385, www.holders.net. The major music, opera, drama, comedy and cabaret festival in the Caribbean. International artistes flock to perform here in front of an enthusiastic audience of locals and visitors, but not all the talent is imported. The setting is unbelievably romantic, in the garden of Holders House overlooking a golf course, with thousands of fairy lights twinkling in the palm trees and among the shrubs. Take a picnic and a bottle of bubbly, it's a great social occasion. Don't forget your umbrella and insect repellent.

Oistins Fish Festival Contact Dan Carter, T428 6738. Held at Easter to celebrate the signing of the Charter of Barbados and the history of this fishing town. There are three days of competitions, parades and demonstrations of fishing skills. Fish-boning is the major competition, the winner being the Queen of the Festival. There are also boat races, the greasy pole and a big street party with live music which goes on until late at night – and of course, lots of fried fish and fish cakes. On Easter Sun there is a **Gospel Festival**. A very popular event attracting thousands of people.

April

Barbados Reggae Festival www.the barbadosreggaefestival.com. Beach parties, cruise parties, concerts and the very popular

Open gardens

In addition to the spectacular gardens open regularly to the public, Barbados possesses numerous private gardens, lovingly tended by their owners, which are only occasionally open to public scrutiny. Look out for the Barbados Horticultural Society's open gardens programme, open 1400-1800 on Sundays in January and February. There are gardens running down to the sea, gardens up in the hills, gardens which have been created by landscape designers and gardens which have just grown over the years like Topsy. Barbados has a fine reputation for horticulture and members of the BHS, which has been in existence since 1928, are very keen on their flowers. Barbados regularly exhibits at the Chelsea Flower Show in London in May and has won many medals, a major achievement given the headache of transporting blooms all the way from the Caribbean to the Northern Hemisphere in pristine condition. The BHS holds its own flower show every year in January or February at its headquarters at Balls Plantation, Christ Church, T4285889, www.horticulturebarbados.com, where it has 12 acres of landscaped gardens.

Reggae on the Hill, open air music from 1100 at Farley Hill National Park.

May

Gospelfest www.barbadosgospelfest.com. Held over Whitsun, the last weekend in May, this international festival attracts gospel singers from the USA, UK and all over the Caribbean. Concerts are held at various locations including Farley Hill National Park. Celtic Festival www.celticfestival barbados.com. A rather unusual festival to be celebrated in the Caribbean, but Barbados attracts Celtic people from around the world for their annual gymanfa-ganu and other events including folk music, street theatre, bagpipes, ceilidhs and Celtic chefs.

July/August

Crop Over Held over 5 weeks from mid-Jul when the sugar cane harvest ends. This is the main festival or carnival, with parades and calypso competitions over the weekend leading up to Kadooment Day (the 1st Mon in Aug), and calypso 'tents' for several weeks beforehand. Your eyes will be blasted with colour by costumed dancers, stilt walkers and masqueraders, your ears blasted with sound by tuk bands, calypso, ringbang and steel pan, and your gut blasted by rum, beer, sun, adrenalin and lack of sleep. The celebrations begin with the ceremonial delivery of the last canes on a brightly coloured dray cart pulled by mules, which are blessed. There is a toast to the sugar workers and the crowning of the King and Queen of the crop (the champion cutter-pilers). Weekly calypso tent shows showcase the latest songs with performances by entertainers and comedians as well as calypsonians. Parties, also known as fetes or bashments, start with after work liming, hotting up around midnight and going on until daybreak. Check with costume bands for their band fetes. The Junior Kadooment Parade and Junior Calypso Monarch Competition gives children a chance to have their own carnival and play 'mas'. Things start to hot up big time with the Pic-O-De-Crop semi finals and Party Monarch Calypso competition. From a line up of 18, 7 competitors are selected to go forward to the finals to compete against the reigning Calypso Monarch. This is held on the East Coast road and combined with the Party Monarch Calypso competition, so a great day is had by all with picnics, music and liming overlooking the Atlantic surf. Following the selection of the King of Pic-O-De-Crop Calypso there is Fore-Day Morning Jump Up, an early morning event

Music

No visitor to Barbados can fail to notice the extent to which music pervades daily life. Whether it is reggae pounding out from a passing ZR van or gospel music being belted out in a church, Bajan rhythm is inescapable. The West Africans dragged to the island as slaves brought with them tastes in music and dance which are still evident today. Bajans are born with the ability to gyrate their hips on the dance floor with energy, rhythm and sex appeal, a skill called 'wukkin up', which tourists spend many happy hours trying to emulate. This intensity of sound and beat has produced many musicians, several of which have become world famous, such as The Mighty Gabby, reggae vocalist and songwriter David Kirton, jazz saxophonist Arturo Tappin, Red Plastic Bag and John King, Krosfyah, Square One and Spice. And then there's Rihanna…

Calypso is the musical form for which Barbados is most famous, although it was originally developed in Trinidad. Calypsonians (or kaisonians, as the more historically minded call them) are the commentators, champions and sometime conscience of the people. This unique musical form, a mixture of African, French and, eventually, British, Spanish and even East Indian influences dates back to Trinidad's first 'shantwell', Gros Jean, late in the 18th century. Since then it has evolved into a popular, potent force, with both men and women (also children, of late) battling for the Calypso Monarch's crown during Crop Over, Barbados' carnival, see page 15. Calypsonians perform in 'tents' (performing halls) in the weeks leading

up to the competition and are judged in Pic-O-De-Crop semi-finals, which hones down the list to seven final contenders who compete against the reigning Calypso king. The season's calypso songs blast from radio stations and sound systems all over the islands and visitors should ask locals to interpret the sometimes witty and often scurrilous lyrics, for they are a fascinating introduction to the state of the nation. Currently, party soca tunes dominate although some of the commentary calypsonians are still heard on the radio. There is also a new breed of 'Rapso' artists, fusing calypso and rap music. Chutney, an Indian version of calypso, is also becoming increasingly popular and is also being fused with soca, to create 'chutney soca'. Mac Fingall is a local calypso singer and entertainer, frequently found at cricket matches (his passion) or the races if he is not MC at Crop Over competitions. His great friend Red Plastic Bag, with whom he has recorded several albums, is also frequently heard around the island. The band which has won most prizes, however, is Krosfyah (formerly called Crossfire), known as the kings of soca and led by Edwin Yearwood, their singer/songwriter who has been a triple crown winner at Crop Over.

Pan music has a shorter history, developing in the 20th century from the tamboo-bamboo bands which made creative use of tins, dustbins and pans plus lengths of bamboo for percussion instruments. By the end of the Second World War some ingenious souls discovered that huge oil drums could

borrowed from Trinidad's carnival. It starts in Bridgetown and heads out to Spring Garden, wear old clothes as a lot of oils and paints get liberally smeared around. Cohobblopot is when the kings and queens of the costume

bands show off their creations and compete for prizes and the titles of King and Queen of the Festival. Kadooment is the grand finale of the carnival, when there is a procession of costume bands through the streets,

be converted into expressive instruments, their top surfaces tuned to all ranges and depths (eg the ping pong, or soprano pan embraces 28 to 32 notes, including both the diatonic and chromatic scales). Aside from the varied pans, steel bands also include a rhythm section dominated by the steel, or iron men.

Reggae is tremendously popular in Barbados and is played everywhere, all day, all night. David Kirton is probably the leading Barbadian modern roots reggae artist, now with several albums under his name since his debut album, *Stranger*, in 1999. Biggie Irie, a huge singer with a rich mahogany voice is credited with being one of the key players in the resurgence of reggae bands in Barbados in the 1990s. Reggae jazz saxophonist Arturo Tappin has played at every jazz and reggae festival in the Caribbean and has toured the world with big name artistes. However, Bajans like to vary their reggae so there is also a fusion of reggae and soca, known as ragga-socca, which has a faster rhythm than reggae but slower than up-tempo soca. Ringbang, created in 1994, is a mixture of all the varied types of Caribbean music with the emphasis on the beat rather than the melody.

Tuk is one of the most traditional forms of folk music, having its origins in slave culture of the 17th century and an important means of expression for the black masses in Barbados. It was banned by the English as subversive; plantation overseers believed that the drums were used to send messages, and it had to wait until after emancipation to resurface

officially. Since the revival of Crop Over in 1974, tuk bands have flourished. The instruments used in a tuk band are the kettle drum, bass drum and tin flute. There are several school tuk bands as it is promoted among the younger generation to preserve the island's cultural heritage. The music is lively, with a pulsating rhythm influenced by British regimental band music as well as African dances. It is 'jump up' music, used at holiday times and carnival for masquerades, when tuk bands travel from village to village, playing popular tunes and inviting audience participation.

Musical groups and choirs include the Barbados Chamber Music Ensemble, the Barbados Symphonia, Sing Out Barbados, the Barbados Festival Choir, Ellerslie Folk Chorale, the Barbados National Youth Orchestra and the Cavite Chorale. There are also numerous gospel groups, including the Nazarene Silvertones, Promise, Gratitude, the New Testament Church of God Chorale, the Wesley Singers, Sister Marshall and Joseph Niles and the Consolers. The Choir of the Cathedral Church of St Michael and All Angels (Bridgetown cathedral) is a mixed choir of boy trebles, sopranos, altos, tenors and basses. They can be heard every Sunday at Choral Matins (1100) and Evensong (1800) and every first and third Sunday of the month at the Sung Eucharist (0900). Three concerts are performed annually, A Festival of Nine Lessons and Carols for Christmas, Harvest Thanksgiving on the Sunday before Ash Wednesday and A Solemn Music for Good Friday.

accompanied by trucks of deafening sound systems and fuelled by alcohol. Membership of a band is not restricted to locals, anyone can join and there is a range of costumes to suit all figures and complexions. 3 very

popular bands are Baje Crop Over Mas Band, www.baje-intl.com, Power X 4 Mas Band, www.powerxfour.com and Ooutraje Fedtival Band, www.ooutraje.com. Wear plenty of sun block and drink lots of water to keep

Literature

Two Barbadian writers whose work has had great influence throughout the Caribbean are the novelist **George Lamming** and the poet **Edward Kamau Brathwaite**. Lamming's first novel, *In The Castle Of My Skin* (1953), a part-autobiographical story of growing up in colonial Barbados, deals with one of the major concerns of anglophone writers: how to define one's values within a system and ideology imposed by someone else. Lamming's treatment of the boy's changing awareness in a time of change in the West Indies is both poetic and highly imaginative. His other books include *Natives Of My Person*, *Season Of Adventure* and *The Pleasures Of Exile*.

Brathwaite is also sensitive to the colonial influence on black West Indian culture. Like Derek Walcott of St Lucia and others he is also keenly aware of the African traditions at the heart of that culture. The questions addressed by all these writers are: who is Caribbean man, and what are his faiths, his language, his ancestors? The experience of teaching in Ghana for some time helped to clarify Brathwaite's response. African religions, motifs and songs mix with West Indian speech rhythms in a style which is often strident, frequently using very short verses. His collections include *Islands*, *Masks* and *Rights Of Passage*.

yourself hydrated and compensate for the alcohol. For more information contact the **National Cultural Foundation**, T417 6610, www.ncf.bb.

Banks International Hockey Festival Hockey is very popular in Barbados and this is the largest field hockey event in the region with teams coming from all over the world to participate. Held at Sir Garfield Sobers Sports Complex, matches held during the day are followed by beach parties, fetes, party cruises and night clubs,

November

Barbados Food and Wine and Rum Festival Takes place over several days in various locations, some events free, some US$5 up to US$250, with cooking demonstrations by eminent chefs, wine tastings with sommeliers and rum tours.

The National Independence Festival of Creative Arts (NIFCA) Plays, concerts and exhibitions in the 4 weeks before Independence on 30 Nov. Competitors work their way up through parish heats to reach the finals at the Frank Collymore Hall in Bridgetown. Contact **The National Cultural Foundation**, T417 6610, www.ncf.bb.

Independence Day Although the actual day is 30 Nov, there are several events during the month commemorating Barbados' independence from Britain in 1966.

Essentials A-Z

Accidents and emergencies
Ambulance T511, **Fire** T311, **Police** T211.
Directory assistance T411.

Customs and duty free
You may take in to Barbados 2 litres of spirits or wine duty free and 2 cartons of cigarettes. Fresh fruit and vegetables, plants, cuttings and seeds are restricted or prohibited, depending on where they've come from, to prevent the transmission of pests and disease.

Electricity
110 volts/50 cycles (US standard). Some houses and hotels also have 240-volt sockets for use with British equipment or adaptors, but take your own, just in case.

Embassies and consulates
For all Barbados embassies and consulates abroad and for foreign embassies and consulates in Barbados, see http://embassy.goabroad.com.

Health
Travel in Barbados poses no health risk to the average visitor provided sensible precautions are taken. It is important to see your GP or travel clinic at least 6 weeks before departure for general advice on any travel risks and necessary vaccinations. Try phoning a specialist travel clinic if your own doctor is unfamiliar with health conditions in the Caribbean. Check with your national health service or health insurance on coverage in the islands and take a copy of your insurance policy with you. Also get a dental check, know your own blood group and if you suffer a long-term condition such as diabetes or epilepsy, obtain a Medic Alert bracelet/necklace (www.medicalert.co.uk). If you wear glasses, take a copy of your prescription.

Vaccinations
It is important to confirm your primary courses and boosters are up to date.
It is also advisable to vaccinate against **tetanus**, **typhoid** and **hepatitis A**. Vaccines sometimes advised are **hepatitis B**, **rabies** and **diphtheria**. **Yellow fever** vaccination is not required unless you are coming directly from an infected country in Africa or South America. Although **cholera** vaccination is largely ineffective, immigration officers may ask for proof of such vaccination if coming from a country where an epidemic has occurred. Check www.who.int for updates.

Health risks
The most common affliction of travellers to any country is probably diarrhoea and the same is true of Barbados. Tap water is good in most areas, but bottled water is widely available and recommended. Diarrhoea may be caused by viruses, bacteria (such as E-coli), protozoal (such as giardia), salmonella and cholera. It may be accompanied by vomiting or by severe abdominal pain. Any kind of diarrhoea responds well to the replacement of water and salts. Sachets of rehydration salts can be bought in most pharmacies and can be dissolved in boiled water. If the symptoms persist, consult a doctor.

There is no malaria but cases of dengue fever have been increasing, so take insect repellent and avoid being bitten as much as possible. Sleep off the ground and use a mosquito net and some kind of insecticide. Remember that DEET (Di-ethyltoluamide) is the gold standard. Apply the repellent every 4-6 hrs but more often if you are sweating heavily. If a non-DEET product is used, check who tested it. Validated products (tested at the London School of Hygiene and Tropical Medicine) include Mosiguard, Non-DEET Jungle formula and non-DEET Autan. If you want to use citronella remember that it must be applied very frequently (ie hourly) to be effective.

The climate is hot; the islands are tropical and protection against the sun will be needed. Do not be deceived by cooling sea breezes. To reduce the risk of sunburn and skin cancer, make sure you pack high-factor sun cream, light-coloured loose clothing and a hat.

Insurance

Private medical insurance is essential as medical treatment in Barbados can be very expensive. Local private clinics provide good treatment. The main government hospital can cope with many types of treatment, but serious cases will mean emergency evacuation, usually to the USA. Make sure you have adequate travel health insurance and accessible funds to cover the cost of any medical treatment abroad and repatriation.

Language

English is the official language although there is a Bajan dialect spoken which incorporates West African languages. Barbados uses British spelling of English.

Money

The currency is the Barbados dollar, B$, which is pegged at B$1.98=US$1. There are notes for B$2, 5, 10, 20, 50 and 100 and coins for B$1, 25 cents, 10 cents, 5 cents and 1 cent. Many tourist establishments quote prices in US dollars, which are widely accepted, although you will get any change in B$. Banks will only change the US and Canadian dollar, euro and sterling.

Plastic/currency cards/Banks (ATMs)

Credit cards are widely used and ATMs are found in supermarkets, shopping centres and some petrol stations as well as banks. Credit and debit cards can be used to withdraw cash, which will be B$. To find a MasterCard ATM, try www.mastercard.co.uk/atm-locator.html. Inform your bank before you travel that you are going to Barbados

so they don't put a stop on your card. Make sure you bring contact details from home of who to call if your card is lost or stolen. If you don't want to carry lots of cash, prepaid currency cards allow you to preload money from your bank account, fixed at the day's exchange rate. They look like a credit or debit card and are issued by specialist money changing companies, such as Travelex and Caxton FX. You can top up and check your balance by phone, online and sometimes by text.

Cost of living/travelling

Barbados is not cheap, but there are ways of making your money go further. Even on a tight budget you will need US$50 per day for food and drink. Eating where Bajans eat for lunch, for instance, will cost you US$5-6, but lunch at a beach bar will cost 2 or 3 times that amount. Stick with local Banks beer (US$2 for 500 ml) rather than imported beers and rum is better value than wine. Self-catering is popular even if it is only for a picnic and the supermarkets are well stocked with familiar brands from North America and some from the UK. Milk costs US$3 per litre and bottled water is US$2.75 for a large (1.5-litre) bottle. Expect to pay US$60 for a 3-course meal for 2 at a mid-range restaurant. Buses are cheap and frequent in the main tourist areas along the south and west coasts into Bridgetown, US$1 per journey, while car hire will cost from US$85 per day. Activities and tours such as a sunset booze cruise start at about US$70, but on the other hand you can do a National Trust hike for free.

Opening hours

Banks open Mon-Thu 0800-1500, Fri 0800-1700. Banks at shopping centres are usually open Mon-Thu 1000-1900 and Fri 1000-2000. Some open Sat 1000-1500. **Shops** are generally open 0900-1700 Mon-Fri, 0900-1300 Sat. **Supermarkets** open earlier and later and some are open on Sun morning.

Post

The General Post Office Headquarters is in Cheapside, Bridgetown and there are district post offices in every parish, open Mon 0800-1500 and Tue-Fri 0800-1515. A Philatelic Bureau issues 1st-day covers 4 times a year.

Public holidays

1 Jan New Year's Day.
21 Jan Errol Barrow Day.
Mar/Apr Good Friday, Easter Monday.
28 Apr National Heroes' Day.
1 May Labour Day.
May/Jun Whit Monday.
1 Aug Emancipation Day.
1st Mon in Aug Kadooment Day.
30 Nov Independence Day.
25 Dec Christmas Day.
26 Dec Boxing Day.

Safety

Take normal precautions against theft. Do not leave your things unattended on the beach, shut windows and lock patio doors at night. There are some areas of Bridgetown, such as Nelson St, you should avoid late at night. Baxters Rd is generally safe although it attracts cocaine addicts (*paros*). Take care when walking along deserted beaches and watch out for pickpockets in tourist areas. If hiring a car, watch out for people who wash the vehicle unasked and then demand money.

Taxes

Departure tax is included in the cost of the air ticket at the point of purchase. VAT on accommodation and direct tourism services (restaurants, car rental, sight entrance fees, activities and tours) was to be reduced to 7.5% from 1 Oct 2013. VAT on other goods and services remains at 17.5%.

Telephone

The IDD code for Barbados is +246. Lime and Digicel are the 2 telephone providers. You can rent mobile phones or SIM cards on arrival from either

company. www.time4lime.com/bb or http://digicelbarbados.com.

Time

Atlantic Standard Time, 4 hrs behind GMT, 1 hr ahead of EST.

Tipping

A 10% service charge is usually added to hotel and restaurant bills, although sometimes you are charged 15% in restaurants. Any additional tip is greatly appreciated. Tips in a restaurant are divided up between all the kitchen staff. In hotels it is customary to leave a tip for the chambermaid. This can be anything from US$5 to US$100 at the luxury establishments.

Tourist information

The Barbados Tourism Authority has its main office in Harbour Rd, Bridgetown (T427 2623, www.visitbarbados.org, also on Facebook, open Mon-Fri 0900-1700). There are also offices at the deepwater harbour (T426 1718) and the airport (T428 0937). Contact details for BTA offices abroad can be found on the website. A good source of information is *Explore Our Isle Barbados*, published and distributed free by *The Nation* daily newspaper and available as an e-guide. *Sporting Barbados* (www.sportingbarbados.com) is another free glossy, plenty of useful information. *Ins and Outs of Barbados*, www.mydestination.com/barbados also free, is published annually, a glossy with lots of historical articles as well as advertizing and useful year-round calendar, distributed by the Barbados Hotel & Tourism Association. Their other publications include *Barbados in a Nutshell*, a pocket guide which comes free with most car rentals, and *Visit Barbados*, usually only available off the island at BTA offices worldwide. All 3 are available as e-guides.

Maps

Ordnance Survey Tourist Maps include Barbados in the series, 1:50,000 scale with inset of Bridgetown 1:10,000, available from the Public Buildings in Bridgetown, from the museum, in the airport and from some bookstores in town. GeoCenter publish a Holiday Map, 1:60,000 scale with inset of Bridgetown, 1:7,500, the Garrison, the west coast and the south coast with sites of tourist interest marked. Esso distributes a road map with the free *Barbados in a Nutshell* booklet (advertising), with insets of Bridgetown, the west coast and the south coast with hotels marked. The Tourism Authority does a useful free leaflet with map for a self-guided walking tour of Bridgetown.

Visas

All visitors must have a passport and a return ticket. Most visitors do not need a visa unless they plan to work or study in Barbados, although the length of stay permitted varies from 28 days to 6 months. For full details and how to apply for a visa if needed, see the Ministry of Foreign Affairs and Foreign Trade website, www.foreign.gov.bb.

State the maximum period you intend to stay on arrival. Overstaying is not recommended if you wish to re-enter Barbados at a later date. Extending your stay is possible by applying to the **Chief Immigration Officer**, Immigration Department, Careenage House on the Wharf in Bridgetown (T426 1011, Mon-Fri 0830-1630); take your passport and return ticket; it's a time consuming procedure.

Contents

Footprint features

Barbados

Bridgetown → *For listings, see pages 63-80.*

The capital, Bridgetown, on the southwest corner of the island is small but busy and full of life. The southern part of the bay is beach, with water sports and nightlife on offer, popular with a young crowd. There are no really large buildings except Tom Adams Financial Centre, which houses the central bank and the Frank Collymore Concert Hall. Swan Street is now a lively pedestrian street where Barbadians do their shopping and street music is sometimes performed. On Broad Street, previously called Cheapside, Exchange Street and New England Street, you will find a whole range of sophisticated shops catering for tourists, with large shopping malls, duty-free shops and department stores. More developments are planned along by the Careenage where old warehouses have been converted for other uses and restaurants overlook boats plying their trade on the inlet. The suburbs sprawl along the south and west coasts, and quite a long way inland. Many of the suburban areas are very pleasant, full of flowering trees and 19th-century coral stone gingerbread villas. There are two interesting areas, downtown Bridgetown with National Heroes Square on the north side of the Careenage and the historic area at Garrison. In 2011, the old town, its port and the Garrison were inscribed as a UNESCO World Heritage Site.

Arriving in Bridgetown

Getting there
The Adams Barrow Cummins (ABC) Highway skirts around the city from the airport in the southeast to the west coast. Several roundabouts along the highway give access into Bridgetown. There is also a road along the south coast, which enters the city through the Garrison Historical Area and a road running down the west coast which comes into the capital as the Spring Gardens Highway. Buses and route taxis run frequently in to and out of town along all these roads.

Getting around
The centre of Bridgetown is easily toured on foot, while buses, route taxis and taxis are available for reaching points a bit further afield.

Tourist information
The Barbados Tourism Authority has its main office in Harbour Road, Bridgetown, T427 2623, www.visitbarbados.org, also on Facebook, open Monday-Friday 0900-1700. There is also an office at the deepwater harbour (cruise ship terminal), T4261718.

Background

Bridgetown was once known as Indian Bridge, after the basic wooden bridge across the Careenage found by the first settlers. It was later called the Town of St Michael, after the parish in which it lies. It is set around Carlisle Bay, with the Deep Water Harbour for cruise and cargo ships to the north and in the middle, an inlet known as the Careenage, at the mouth of Constitution River, where schooners and other trading vessels used to tie up. It got its name because the schooners were careened onto their sides so that the hulls could be cleaned or mended. Nowadays, small craft such as catamarans and sport fishing boats tout their wares to visitors, overlooked by restaurants with a dominant nautical theme.

Places in Central Bridgetown

National Heroes Square
National Heroes Square, a small, triangular 'square', is the hub of central Bridgetown. It was called Trafalgar Square until 1999 and there is a statue there of Lord Nelson, sculpted by Sir Richard Westmacott and predating its London equivalent by 30 years. Admiral Nelson visited Barbados with his fleet in 1805, a few months before his death, and the square was named in 1806, with the statue being erected in 1813. The name has recently been the subject of some controversy as it was thought to link Barbados too closely with its colonial past. After more than 30 years of independence, the Little England jibes were a trifle past their sell by date. Nelson was turned through 180° so that he no longer looked down Broad Street, the main shopping area, and there was talk of him being moved, but no suitable home was found. The square now celebrates ten official national heroes, including Sir Grantley Adams. There is a memorial to the Barbadian war dead and the fountain commemorates the piping of water to Bridgetown in 1861.

To the north are the neo-Gothic **Parliament Buildings**. The **West Building** was built in 1871 and the **East Building** was finished in 1874. They are imposing grey buildings with a red roof and green shutters. The **clock tower** on the west wing dates from 1886, the original having been demolished, and now houses public offices. The East Building, housing the Senate and the House of Assembly, has stained-glass windows depicting British kings and queens from James I to Queen Victoria and even includes Oliver Cromwell. You can walk between the buildings (providing you are correctly dressed).

Chamberlain Bridge

Running south from the square is Chamberlain Bridge, for centuries one of the capital's two main bridges and built roughly in the same place as the old Indian Bridge. In 1872 it was a steel swing bridge and it was given its present name at the beginning of the 20th century in honour of Joseph Chamberlain, British Colonial Secretary, who gave the island a large chunk of money in grants and loans to keep the economy afloat. In 2005 it

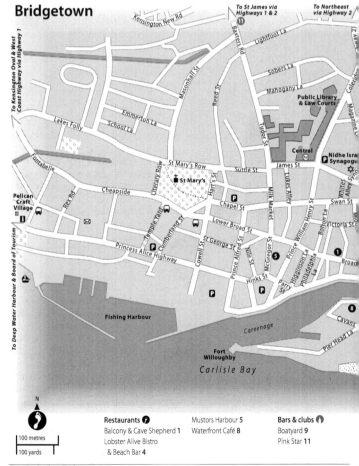

Bridgetown

Restaurants 🍴
Balcony & Cave Shepherd **1**
Lobster Alive Bistro
& Beach Bar **4**

Mustors Harbour **5**
Waterfront Café **8**

Bars & clubs 🍸
Boatyard **9**
Pink Star **11**

was demolished when bits started falling off it and it was rebuilt using modern materials: fibre-reinforced plastic, which is long-lasting, lightweight and non-corrosive. It reopened in 2006 as a lift bridge adjoining the coral stone arch structure dating from 1861, which was refurbished. There is a plaque with the Barbados National Anthem on the bridge, **Independence Arch**, at the southern end of the bridge, was built in 1987 to celebrate 21 years of independence.

Charles Duncan O'Neal Bridge

The second bridge, going off southeast from the square, is the Charles Duncan O'Neal Bridge, named after one of the founding fathers of democracy in Barbados (1879-1936) and a national hero. The old bridge was pulled down in 1967 and replaced with a wider, stronger, modern structure to take the increased volume of vehicular traffic. If you are driving, the junctions can be a bit scary until you get the hang of the one-way system as locals drive very fast over the river and away. The market and one of the bus stations create extra hazards on the south side of the bridge.

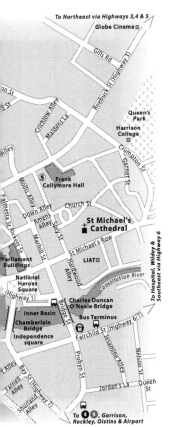

St Michael's Cathedral

Take the northeast exit out of National Heroes Square along St Michael's Row to reach the 18th-century Anglican St Michael's Cathedral. It has a fine set of inscriptions and a single-hand clock. The first building was consecrated in 1665 but destroyed by a hurricane in 1780. The present cathedral is long and broad with a balcony. It has a fine vaulted ceiling, at one time the widest in the world, and some tombs (1675) have been built into the porch. Completed in 1789 with £10,000 raised in a lottery, it became a cathedral in 1825 with the arrival of Bishop Coleridge, but suffered hurricane damage in 1831. Both Sir Grantley Adams and his son, Tom Adams, both prime ministers, are buried here along with other famous Barbadians.

Queen's Park and around

If you continue east, you reach **Queen's Park**, a pleasant, restful park just outside the city centre, with the largest tree in Barbados: a 28-m baobab with a circumference of 25 m, thought to be over 1000 years old. Baobabs originated in Guinea and it is thought the see floated across the Atlantic

Geography

Barbados is 21 miles long and 14 miles wide, lying east of the main chain of the Leeward and Windward islands. Most of the island is covered by a cap of coral limestone, up to 600,000 years old. Several steep inland cliffs or ridges run parallel to the coast. These are the remains of old shorelines, which formed as the island gradually emerged from the sea. There are no rivers in this part of the island, although there are steep-sided gullies down which water runs in wet weather. Rainwater runs through caves in the limestone, one of which, Harrison's Cave, has been developed as a tourist attraction. The island's water supply is pumped up from the limestone. In the Scotland District in the northeast, the coral limestone has been eroded and older, softer rocks are exposed. There are rivers here, which have cut deep, steep-sided valleys.

and grew on the edge of a lagoon. The park and its fountain were designed by Lady Gilbert Carter, the wife of the Governor, who opened the gates in 1909 with a golden key. **Queen's Park House**, a beautiful building dating from 1786, was once the residence of the General commanding the British troops in the West Indies. It was known as King's House until Queen Victoria came to the throne, and in the 20th century became a small theatre (Daphne Joseph-Hackett Theatre) and art gallery. However, both have closed in recent years because of deterioration of the structure and the house is now boarded up.

Further east still is **Government House**, first known as Pilgrim House. It was purchased for the Government in 1736 from John Pilgrim, a Quaker, as the permanent residence of the Governor. It is a typical example of a plantation Great House, with arched porticoes, jalousie window shutters, verandas, a parapet roof and a circular driveway, as well as delightful gardens. It is included in the Barbados National Trust's Open Houses programme, when you can have a guided tour for US$15.

Nidhe Israel Synagogue and museum
ⓘ *Synagogue Lane, T436 6869, see Facebook, Mon-Fri, 0900-1600.*
This is an early 19th-century building on the site of a 17th-century one, one of the two earliest in the Western hemisphere. The original synagogue was built in the 1660s by Jews fleeing Recife, Brazil, who heard that Oliver Cromwell had granted freedom of worship for Jews and gained permission to settle in Barbados. Cromwell granted the first pass to settle in 1655 to Dr Abraham de Mercado, an elder of the Recife society and his son David Rafael. Jews in Barbados were granted the right to worship publicly even before Jews in London, and Barbados was the first British possession to grant Jews full political rights at the beginning of the 19th century. Recently painstakingly restored, the synagogue is now used for religious services again and is open to visitors.

Coleridge Street
In a block along Coleridge Street are the **Public Library**, founded by Andrew Carnegie, the **Law Courts** and the **Central Police Station**. At one time the Legislature, the Law Courts and the jail were on this site, leading Henry Nelson Coleridge to write in 1832: "His Majesty's Council, the General Assembly, the Judge, the juries, the debtors and the felons, all live together in the same house". On the other side of the road opposite the library, is the **Montefiore fountain**. It was built as a drinking water fountain in 1864 by

Barbados' barmy army

Barbados is an island and you would expect it to have a navy. It does, but it's a navy that never goes to sea. Barbados is the only country to have a 'landship' movement. Founded in the 1860s by a retired seaman, Moses Wood, and his friends, it was an attempt to recreate the camaraderie that Bajan sailors missed when they returned to their native land after working all their lives afloat. The fleet is commanded by an Admiral and has incorporated all the ratings of the British Navy. The crew of the Barbados Landship (Her Majesty's Landship before

Independence) wears navy-style uniforms and uses the language of 'Jack Tars'. The landship attends church services, parades and festivals such as Crop Over with their corps of drum (a tuk band). Dancers make up the outline of a ship and each has a special role to play, with the admiral on the bridge, sailors scrubbing the decks and the tuk band as the engine. Their marching/dancing parodies the parades of real navies with names like 'the Changing of the Guard', 'Admiral's Inspection' and 'Rough Seas' – certainly the navy with the best sense of rhythm in the world.

John Montefiore in memory of his father, a leading merchant who died of cholera, and was originally in Beckwith Place, Lower Broad Street. It was moved to Coleridge Street in 1940 and there is no water connected to it. The statues on each face of the monument represent Justice, Fortitude, Temperance and Prudence.

Bay Street

Bay Street runs south of the city centre hugging the edge of **Carlisle Bay**, which is a surprisingly good beach considering how close it is to town. Yachts anchor here, snorkelling and diving parties call in and there are beach facilities, umbrellas, sunbeds, food, drink and parking at the Boatyard. Hugely popular are the water trampoline and the inflatable water slide which looks like an iceberg. A lively place, lots of action, always something going on, often packed with cruise ship visitors. A marine reserve has been created here with a series of interlocking underwater marine trails, the park being roughly marked out underwater by old cannon, anchors and pylons leading the way from one wreck to the next. There are six shallow wrecks, some of them suitable for snorkellers. One of the wrecks is the Cornwallis, which was torpedoed in 1942 by a German U boat; the hull was moved from deeper water in Carlisle Bay into the shallower Marine Reserve. Another is the Bajan Queen, a tugboat converted to a party boat before being sunk in 2002. She sits only a few metres underwater, perfect for snorkelling or diving, and is growing a variety of coral as well as being home to plenty of fish.

St Patrick's Cathedral ① *Bay St, at the corner of Jemmotts Lane, St Michael, T426 2325*, is the Roman Catholic cathedral, started in 1840 but not long built before it was gutted by fire in 1897. The current building dates from 1899 and was built through subscriptions and donations from the Government and people from all faiths, Protestants and Jews as well as Catholics. It became a cathedral in 1970.

Places in the Garrison Historic Area

South of central Bridgetown is the Garrison area on the strategic southeast point guarding the entrance to Carlisle Bay and the capital. In the face of a possible French invasion in 1785,

Bim volumes

In addition to being called Little England, Barbados is frequently referred to affectionately as 'Bim' or 'Bimshire'. In the 1960s the musical of Barbados, *Ballad for Bimshire*, was staged in New York, with lyrics by Irving Burgie, who also wrote the words for the Barbados National Anthem. The Barbados Museum houses a permanent exhibition on Amerindian life called 'In Search of Bim'. Austin Clarke, winner of the Canadian 2002 Giller Prize, set his novel, *The Polished Hoe*, in the post-colonial West Indian island of Bimshire. The literary magazine, *Bim*, launched numerous Bajan and West Indian authors under its most influential editor, Frank Collymore. There's even an internet chat room for Bajans called Club Bimshire.

a permanent garrison was built as the headquarters of the British army in the region. The 64-acre site adjacent to Charles Fort and St Ann's Fort is now the Garrison Historic Area. Surrounding the parade ground, now the six-furlong race course, are numerous 17th- to 19th-century military buildings constructed from brick brought as ballast on ships from England. They are built on traditional British colonial lines, examples of which can be seen throughout the Caribbean and in India. Painted bright colours, some now contain government offices. There are several memorials around the oval race course. In the southwest corner is one commemorating the 'awful' hurricane which killed 14 men and one married woman and caused the destruction of the barracks and hospital on 18 August 1831, and outside the Barbados Museum in the northeast corner there's another to the men of the Royal York Rangers who fell in action against the French in Martinique, Les Saintes and Guadeloupe in the 1809-1810 campaign. **The Savannah**, now a race course, is used at other times for early morning or evening jogging, exercising the horses, informal rugby and basketball games and there's usually something going on on Sunday afternoons.

Fort Charles and St Anne's Fort

Fort Charles on Needham Point, was the largest of the many which guarded the south and west coasts. It forms part of the gardens of the Hilton Hotel. Only the ramparts remain but there are a number of 24 pounder cannon dating from 1824. The oil refinery was the site of the naval dockyard. Built in 1805, it was subsequently moved to English Harbour, Antigua. The buildings were then used as barracks before being destroyed in the 1831 hurricane. The military cemetery was the burial ground for the Garrison and the headstones make interesting reading. It appears, for instance that disease claimed more lives than military action.

St Anne's Fort is still used by the Barbados defence force. You cannot enter but look for the crenellated signal tower with its flag pole on top. It formed the high command of a chain of signal posts, the most complete of which is at Gun Hill (see page 33). The long, thin building is the old drill hall.

The Main Guard

The Main Guard, overlooking the savannah, has a nice old clock tower and a fine wide veranda. It has been turned into an information centre and houses exhibits about the West Indian Regiment. The **Garrison Secretary of the Regiment** ① *T426 0982*, is here. It is also a good place from where to watch the horse racing. Races go clockwise. Outside is the **National Cannon Collection**, an impressive array of about 30 cannon, some are mounted

Patriotic titbits

The National Flag of Barbados is made up of three vertical panels, the two on the outside are ultramarine blue, representing the sea and the sky, while the middle panel is gold for the sun and the sand. In the gold panel is a black broken trident, which appears in the seal of the colony, later replaced by the Barbados Coat of Arms. The broken shaft represents the country's break with its colonial status.

The 10 National Heroes are Sir Grantley Adams (1898-1971), Errol Barrow (1920-1987), Bussa (died 1816), Sarah Ann Gill (1795-1866), Charles Duncan O'Neal (1879-1936), Clement Payne (1904-1941), Samuel Jackman Prescod (1806-1871), Sir Garfield Sobers (1936-), Sir Hugh Worrell Springer (1913-1994), Sir Frank Walcott (1916-1999).

The National Flower of Barbados is the Pride of Barbados (Dwarf Poinciana or Flower Fence). Although several colour variations can be found, the red variety with the yellow margin is accepted as the National Flower and appears on the Coat of Arms.

on metal 'garrison' gun carriages (replaced with wooden ones during action as they were prone to shatter). There are also a number of newer howitzers, dating from 1878. The late Major Mike Hartland collected many of the cannon on display.

Barbados Museum

ⓘ *T427 0201/436 1956, www.barbmuse.org.bb. US$7.50 for adults, Mon-Sat 0900-1700, Sun 1400-1800, library available for research purposes.*

This museum is housed in the old military prison on the northeast corner of the savannah. Based on a collection left by Rev N B Watson (late rector of St Lucy Parish), it is all well set out through a series of 10 galleries. It displays natural history, local history (in search of *Bim*), a fine map gallery including the earliest map of Barbados by Richard Ligon (1657), colonial furniture (Plantation House Rooms), military history (including a reconstruction of a prisoner's cell), prints and paintings which depict social life in the West Indies, decorative and domestic arts (17th- to 19th-century glass, china and silver), Africa and its people in the Caribbean, a children's gallery and one to house temporary exhibits. Photography is banned. If the fans aren't working, the rather dark galleries can be humid and oppressive. The museum shop has a good selection of craft items, books, prints, and cards.

George Washington House

ⓘ *Bush Hill, The Garrison, T228 5461, www.georgewashingtonbarbados.org, Mon-Fri 0900-1630, closed Sep, US$10, children US$2.50.*

Otherwise known as Bush Hill House, this is where the future first president of the USA stayed in 1751 for a few months when, as a 19-year-old, he accompanied his sick brother Lawrence (who later died) to search for a cure for his TB. This was George Washington's only excursion outside his homeland and Bridgetown was the largest town he had seen. At that time, Barbados was a more advanced society than that of America, with better health care. Washington was introduced to the delights of the theatre as well as banquets and fine dining, where he met the leading scientists, engineers and military strategists of the day. He contracted smallpox but the skill of a British doctor saved him. As a result of his brush with death, he acquired immunity to the virus which enabled him to survive an outbreak of the disease during the American War of Independence which killed many of his men. The house has been beautifully restored and you can see a video as well as have a guided tour.

Mallalieu Motor Collection
ⓘ *Pavilion Court, Hastings Rd (Highway 7), T426 4640, US$10, Mon-Fri 0900-1700, or Sat-Sun by appointment.*
Bill Mallalieu opened his collection of vintage cars to the public: the Mallalieu Motor Collection. It boasts a 1947 Bentley, Daimler, Humber, Vanden Plas Princess, Wolseley, Lanchester and many others. Every car has a story to tell and Bill is a great raconteur. He is usually there in the mornings. The old cars are often used in processions such as the Holetown Festival, escorting Miss Holetown and other personalities.

Around Bridgetown

The **Harry Bayley Observatory** ⓘ *Clapham, St Michael, not far from Banks Brewery, T424 5593, Fri 2030-2330, US$5, children US$2.50,* is operated by the Barbados Astronomical Society, which opens it to the public once a week. It is the only observatory in the Eastern Caribbean and is a chance for northern visitors to look through a 14-inch reflector telescope at the Southern Hemisphere stars and planets, which aren't all visible from North America and Europe.

Tyrol Cot Heritage House and Craft Village
ⓘ *Codrington Hill, St Michael, T424 2074, Mon-Fri 0800-1630, last tour 1600, US$5.75, children US$2.90.*
Built in 1854 by William Farnum, this attraction is preserved for posterity by the National Trust for being the home, from 1929, of Sir Grantley Adams, the founder of the Barbados Labour Party, Prime Minister of the short-lived West Indies Federation and of the newly independent Barbados. It was also the birthplace of his son, Tom Adams, who was Prime Minister in 1976-1985. The house is built of coral stone and ballast bricks and is furnished with mahogany pieces. There is a Heritage Village with craftsmen at work, plus chattel-house museum, gardens and rum shop. To get there, from the ABC Highway take the Green Hill turning off the Everton Weekes roundabout, continue until you reach the traffic lights at a crossroads near the National Stadium. The entrance is in the white stone wall on the right.

Brandons and Brighton beach
Just north of the town centre are Brandons Beach and Brighton Beach, the latter being home to the **Cockspur Beach Club** ⓘ *Black Rock, St Michael, T425 9393, see Facebook, Mon-Fri 0900-1700, general admission US$10, children US$5; lunch package US$40, children US$20; credit cards accepted,* attached to the **West Indies Rum Distillery** ⓘ *T425 9301, www.westindiesrum.com, US$2.50.* There are guided tours of the distillery, which has been in operation since 1893 and makes Cockspur and Malibu rums, but you can also opt for a day on the beach, taking advantage of the watersports on offer, the bar and live music. Beach chairs, umbrellas and changing facilities are available on any package, but if you go for the lunch pass you receive transport to and from your hotel. Book a day in advance. Malibu, a rum and coconut mix is apparently one of the fastest growing spirits in the world. Less well known is the Malibu Lime, a blend of white rum and lime which is only available in Barbados and France.

Karl 'Broodie' Broodhagen (1909-2002)

Karl Broodhagen was the major sculptor in Barbados and although he was born in Guyana of Dutch, Portuguese and African ancestry, he had lived in Barbados since he was a teenager and came to be considered a son of the soil. He started out life as a tailor, but was obsessed with clay and plaster sculpture. After an exhibition at the British Council in 1948 he received a scholarship to study at Goldsmith's College in London, where he received his formal training. His work concentrated on portraits of people, exploring the strength of character of the individual. Fine examples of this investigation of the inner person include his busts of eminent Barbadians such as the author George Lamming, Frank Collymore and Dame Nita Barrow, although he created busts of most of the people who have transformed Barbadian society into what it is today. One of his major works is a larger than life bronze bust of Sir Grantley Adams, bent and brooding at the end of his life, but the statue he is best known for is the *Slave in Revolt*, familiarly known as 'Bussa', a 305-cm bronze unveiled in 1985. You can see this atop the roundabout on the ABC Highway, leaving Bridgetown on Two Mile Hill. The slave appears to be rising up from a crouched position, the chains on his wrists broken as though he has been freed from slavery but not totally released from bondage. In April 2002, a major work by Broodie, a joint effort with his son, Virgil, was unveiled. This too is on a roundabout on the ABC Highway named in honour of Sir Garfield Sobers and is of the great cricketer himself, a larger than life one and a half tonne statue of the country's living National Hero.

St George Parish Church

ⓘ *Highway 4B, T436 8794, www.anglican.bb.*

One of the oldest churches on the island, it was one of only four parish churches to escape the 1831 hurricane when so many were damaged. Inside there is a magnificent altar painting of the Resurrection by Benjamin West, the first American president of the Royal Academy, and there are statues and other sculpture, including work by Richard Westmacott, the creator of the statue of Lord Nelson in Heroes Square, Bridgetown.

Gun Hill Signal Station

ⓘ *Fusilier Rd, Gun Hill, T429 1358, Mon-Sat 0900-1700, US$5.*

The approach is by Fusilier road and you will pass the Lion carved by British soldiers in 1868 and then turn left to the Signal Station. The road was built by Royal Scot Fusiliers between September 1862 and February 1863 when they were stationed at Gun Hill to avoid yellow fever. The signal station itself had its origins in the slave uprising of 1816. It was decided that a military presence would be maintained outside Bridgetown in case of further slave uprisings. It was also intended for advance warning of attack from the sea and has a commanding view of the whole of the south coast across to Bridgetown harbour. The chain of six signal stations on the island was intended to give very rapid communications with the rest of the island but was soon superseded by the telephone. The hexagonal tower had two small barrack rooms attached and would have been surrounded by a pallisade. The signal stations quickly lost importance as military installations but provided useful information about shipping movements. Gun Hill has been fully restored and there are now lots of royal connections, with visits from Prince Edward, Princess Margaret and

Princess Alexandra all commemorated in photos. Prince Edward planted a tree in 1987 and came back to check on it in 1992. Informative guides will explain the workings of the signal station and point out interesting features of the surrounding countryside.

Orchid World

ⓘ *Groves, St George, T433 0774, www.orchid worldbarbados.com, open 0900-1700, US$12.50, gift shop, snack bar, toilets, wheelchair accessible, the Sergeant St bus from Fairchild Terminal, Bridgetown, stops outside the entrance.*

Some 30,000 orchids are grown in this six-acre orchid garden in a beautiful, mind-blowing display, don't miss this. They come from all over the world, some being grown in full sun, trained on wire fences so their roots don't touch the ground, some grown on trees, some in the ground, some in coconut shells and some in 'houses' for partial shade under nets. A path meanders down the hillside, initially through woodland, where orchids and other plants grow in their natural environment. Then you come out onto lawns where the path is directed between living fences of orchids, before you are bombarded with visual splendour in the orchid houses. The colours are breathtaking, words can not describe the range and variety, each one seeming better than anything seen before. There are plants for sale and the gift shop will sell you orchids on tea towels, trays, mugs and numerous other souvenirs.

West Coast → *For listings, see pages 63-80.*

Known as the Platinum Coast with luxury hotels and villas along the seafront, the west is not just for posh pensioners and well-heeled celebrities. Low-key elegance is the order of the day and standards are very high. Good quality accommodation, at the cheaper end of the market, can also be found if you take time to look and are prepared to walk a few minutes to the beach. The road north of Bridgetown on Highway 1 is wall-to-wall low-rise, intimate hotels and villas, running through Fitts Village, Holetown, Speightstown and up to Little Good Harbour, punctuated by some excellent places to eat. North of Speightstown the coast is quieter and less developed with fishing villages rather than holiday resorts. Highway 2A runs parallel inland and goes through the sugar cane heartland, giving access to tourist sights on this side of the island. Most of the west coast is a golden sand beach, even the towns of Speightstown and Holetown have tempting sandy areas which are clean and attractive. Access can be tricky where there is solid development between the road and the sea, but look out for footpaths between hotels where you can get down to the water without tackling an officious hotel doorman. All beaches are public, but some hotels and restaurants block you out by cramming the narrow strip of sand with their sun beds or denying access through their property. The beaches are narrow, particularly in areas with greatest erosion, but the sea is usually calmer than elsewhere, if a little uncomfortable underfoot due to broken bits of coral.

Turtles

Several turtle-watching tours are on offer as part of a day-sail to the area around Alleynes Bay and Gibbs Beach, where groups of them can be found. Unfortunately, the crews of the ships feed the turtles and fish to attract them to the boats, a practice which encourages aggressive species of fish and upsets the balance of nature. Individual turtles can also be found at snorkelling spots on the south coast. The hawksbill frequently nests on local beaches July to October, the leatherback occasionally in February to June. Green turtles are occasionally found in Bajan waters.

Bridgetown to Holetown

Batts Rock and Paradise Beach

About 1 km north of the roundabout where Highway 1 begins, turn sharp left. Drive down to **Batts Rock Beach**, walk south to get to **Paradise Beach**. Batts Rock has a car park, trees for shade, children's playground, picnic tables, shower and changing facilities. Work on a new **Four Seasons** hotel and luxury villa development at Paradise Beach was held up for several years, leaving an unfinished building site, but it appears that work will soon restart. Meanwhile, the beach is beautiful, with calm water and many cruise ship visitors come here for the day. Swimming and snorkelling is good at both Batts Rock and Paradise Beach and there are often turtles to swim with. You can keep going south along the shoreline as far as Deepwater Harbour, a nice walk, mostly beach.

Paynes Bay

Paynes Bay is quite a wide sweep of pale golden sand (for the west coast) with trees at one end and crystal clear water for swimming. Surfboards and other watersports can be arranged, all very casual and relaxed. Snorkelling is good here as the reef is quite close in to shore. For US$20 you can go out on a glass bottomed boat with snorkelling gear to swim over a wreck and spot turtles. Catamarans also come here to see the turtles, but they don't like crowds. The best time to see them is when there are few people in the water and then they often approach and are quite curious. It is a long swim out to the turtle area so you need to be a strong swimmer. There is access to the beach at several points but parking is limited. Try the roadside just south of Sandy Lane where the trees give shade and a path leads down to the beach, otherwise park a bit further south.

Sandy Lane Hotel

ⓘ *T444 2000, www.sandylane.com.*

This hotel was first opened in 1961 by Ronald Tree, whose own beach house, Heron Bay, could no longer accommodate all the rich and famous people who wanted to stay there. Sandy Lane was immediately known for attracting a wealthy clientele and its name is synonymous with luxury. It is an institution in Barbados and you can't miss it as you drive up Highway 1, through the gracious avenue of ancient trees, passing its grand entrance on the sea side of the road and the golf course on the inland side. Countless film stars, politicians and dignitaries have stayed there and it soon built up a huge list of repeat guests fleeing winter in the Northern Hemisphere for a spot of pampering in the tropical sunshine. However, there was a change of ownership in 1996 and after

The pirate of good position

Stede Bonnet was an unlikely pirate, having been born into a prosperous planter family in Barbados. He became a major in the island militia, a magistrate and plantation owner, never short of a bob or two particularly after his advantageous marriage to a local heiress. However, for some unexplained reason he jacked the whole lot in, bought a sloop with 10 guns, recruited a pirate crew of 70 and set off for the High Seas.

A series of colourful escapades brought him international renown and a brief partnership with the fearsome Edward Teach, also known as Blackbeard. His downfall came after several raids along the New England coast. Two warships were sent to capture him and bring him to justice. The 'pirate of good position' was later hanged, but went down in history as the only pirate to have bought his own ship.

a period of reflection and planning, the hotel was closed for several years. It reopened in March 2001, having been rebuilt, rather than refurbished. Instead of the previous understated elegance so loved of its regular guests, it was considered rather overblown and pretentious, aiming to be the world's premier luxury resort. It is the sort of place where they unpack and pack your suitcase for you and a butler caters to your every need. Beach attendants make sure there isn't a grain of sand on your towel and even polish your sunglasses for you. The old aficionados decamped to other hotels, while a number of travel journalists were banned for what they said about the place, but it appealed to a different clientele: the rich, the famous, the celebrities. Rack rates start from US$1000 a night. Golf has always been a big thing at Sandy Lane, and it runs three golf courses with its own desalination plant for watering the greens and fairways and keeping the five man-made lakes full. The old nine-hole course dates from 1961 and the two new 18-hole courses have been designed by Tom Fazio: **Country Club** and **Green Monkey**, built on former sugar cane land and an old quarry. Look out for the real green monkeys which live in the trees and gullies. If you can't afford to stay here, it is worth going to the **L'Acajou** French restaurant or **Bajan Blue** for the Sunday brunch buffet just to see the place (good food and not all that expensive), but you have to book ahead to get past the gate.

Holetown

Holetown today is a thoroughly modern town but was the place where the earliest settlers landed on 17 February 1627. The Holetown monument commemorates Captain John Powell claiming the island for England and the first landing of Englishmen from the Olive Blossom in July 1605. A secondary plaque marks the 350th anniversary of the first permanent settlement in 1627. Initially named Jamestown, it was renamed Holetown because of a tidal hole near the beach. It was quite heavily defended until after the Napoleonic Wars. Little trace of the forts can be seen now.

Places in Holetown

One of the newest attractions in Barbados is not an adventure sport or a renovated historical mansion, but a shopping centre in Holetown at the junction with First Street. Wanting to present itself as more than just a mall, it is called the **Limegrove Lifestyle Centre** containing, in addition to luxury designer outlets, restaurants, a central bar, a

Barbados

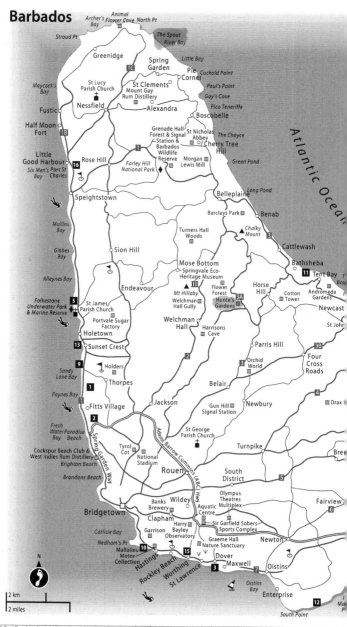

Rocks
Bath
  Conset Bay
Coach Hill □ Codrington College
  Bell Pt
  East Point Lighthouse Ragged Pt
Stewart Hill
  Marley Vale
ttage Vale
Robinsons
  Bottom Bay
unbury antation
  ■ Sam Lord's Castle
  Long Bay
ross' ds
□ Foursquare Rum Factory & Heritage Park
  The Crane
  The Horse
  6
  Crane Bay
  Foul Bay
Salt Cave Pt

cinema complex and art gallery, as well as a spa. They are even building apartments and town houses for those who can't drag themselves away. Shops are open Monday-Saturday 1000-1900, Sunday 1000-1700, restaurants and cafés will provide you with breakfast, lunch, tea and dinner and are open much later. **The Lime Bar** has become one of the places to see and be seen, particularly for weekend nightlife and there is live music Saturday nights.

There is a small shopping centre on the main road, with a supermarket, bank and other services. The **police station**, **post office** ① *Mon 0800-1500, Tue-Fri 0800-1515*, and small **museum** ① *not always open, staff shortages*, are on the other side of the road, with beach access between the police station and the **Tropical Sunset** (formerly Sunswept) Hotel. The sand is swept every morning while the early risers are jogging or walking their dogs. Holetown is overloaded with restaurants and bistros and even with a two-week stay here you'd be pushed to try them all. Most of them are along 1st Street and 2nd Street, convenient to stroll along and see what takes your fancy. Just south of the shopping centre is the Chattel Village, a group of replica traditional chattel houses, all brightly painted, containing boutiques, a gourmet food shop, paper shop and café. South again is Sunset Crest, another shopping area with a small fruit and veg market, an excellent internet café and banks. During the **Holetown Festival** in February, see page 14, the roadside along this stretch of Highway 1 is crammed with people attracted by an open air market for arts and crafts, helped along with tempting local food and drink, while the road itself is a parade ground.

St James Church ① *Holetown, St James, north end of town, over the bridge on the left, www.stjames.truepath.com, open for sightseeing tours Mon-Fri 0900-1300, Sun services 0715, 0800, 0900*, was originally built of wood in 1628. It was replaced by a light coral stone structure in 1680. This building

Chattel houses

Dating from the days of slavery, chattel houses are a distinctive part of Barbados' architectural and social heritage. These wooden houses all conformed to a basic, symmetrical plan, with a central door and a window either side, built on a foundation of loosely packed stones which allowed the air to circulate under and through the house. The steeply pitched roof would have originally been thatched but later they were all galvanized. Each chattel house was customized by its owners, who added pretty shutters, porches, jalousie windows, verandas and decorative detail such as gingerbread fretwork. The key feature of all chattel houses was that they could all be dismantled and moved easily, so that if a worker moved from one plantation to another he could pack up and move with 'all his goods and chattels'.

was extended 20 ft west in 1874 when columns and arches were added and the nave roof raised. You can see the original baptismal font (1684) under the belfry and in the north porch is the original bell of 1696. Many of the original settlers are buried here (although the oldest tombstone of William Balston who died in 1659 is in the Barbados Museum). Church documents dating to 1693 have been removed to the Department of Archives. There are several photos of registers, with many deaths attributed to the small pox epidemic of 1695-1696. There is a lovely stained-glass window depicting the Ascension, which was dedicated in 1924 in memory of the fallen in the First World War and paid for with public donations of B$400. The church was beautifully restored between 1983-1986. On the front pew is a plaque to the President of the USA and Mrs Reagan, who worshipped here on Easter Sunday 11 April 1982.

Folkestone Underwater Park and Marine Reserve ⓘ *Holetown, St James, behind the church, T422 2314, daily 0900-1700, picnic tables under the trees, parking in the shade, children's playground*, was closed for refurbishment in 2013 while a new boardwalk, bathrooms and other facilities were built, although you could still swim and a lifeguard was on duty. What is now Folkestone, was once part of Porter's Plantation, owned for several generations by the Alleyne family, who were stalwart members of the plantocracy and political elite. The 18th-century Folkestone House was marked on the 1825 Barrallier map and was built for the Alleyne family. The name celebrates the marriage in 1751 of Rebecca Alleyne (born 1725) to the Honourable William Bouverie, second Lord Folkestone, and was previously known as Church Point House. The Marine Reserve stretches for 2 km from Coral Reef to Sandy Lane Hotel, including Dottin's Reef and Vauxhall Reef, but here at Folkestone Park you can snorkel in a large area enclosed by buoys. The reef is not in pristine condition but it is surprisingly rewarding as there are quite a lot of fish and you may see turtles. The hawksbill turtle frequently nests on local beaches from July to October, while leatherbacks are occasionally found nesting from February to June. Catamaran tours come up from Bridgetown for snorkelling sessions with the turtles just north of here at Alleyne's Bay. The beach is not great at Folkestone but it is always crowded with people taking advantage of safe swimming and snorkelling in the cordoned off sea. Weekends are busy with families bringing enormous picnics and barbeques, cheerfully setting up home around a picnic bench. There is a life guard and the usual vendors and hair braiders, but no hassling. Glass bottomed boats take you over the reef to two small wrecks further down the coast for US$20 per person.

Around Holetown

East of Holetown there is a clutch of attractions either side of Highway 2, which make a pleasant day trip away from the beach.

Sir Frank Hutson Sugar Machinery Museum

ⓘ *Inland beside the Portvale Sugar Factory off Highway 2A, north of Lawrence Johnson roundabout and parish church of St Thomas, T432 0100, 0900-1700, Mon-Sat although it may be best to call in advance to make sure that the retired worker who staffs it is there, US$7.50 when factory is running Feb-May, US$4 the rest of the time, children half price.*

This museum is in the old buildings beside the sugar factory and is one of those special places which looks unprepossessing but is a treasure trove if you delve into it. Sir Frank Hutson amassed this large collection of machinery and the National Trust now administers it. The exhibition on the story of sugar and its products is fascinating for anyone interested in the history of Barbados but a guided tour is recommended. During the cane-grinding season you can visit the factory to see sugar being produced. The displays are old and worn, while the buildings are also in need of repair, but it can still be fascinating.

Welchman Hall Gully

ⓘ *T438 6671, www.welchmanhallgullybarbados.com, daily, 0900-1630, last tour at 1600, US$12, booklet included, 5-12s US$6, government buses from main terminal in Bridgetown or private buses from Lower Green terminal, all going to Sturges, the former drop you at the back of the gully, leaving you with a 1-km walk, the latter drop you nearer the entrance.*

This gully has a fascinating walk through one of the deep ravines so characteristic of this part of Barbados. You are at the edge of the limestone cap which covers most of the island to a depth of about 100 m. Owned by the National Trust, a good path leads for about half a mile through six sections, each with a slightly different theme. The first section has a devil tree, a stand of bamboo and a judas tree. Next you will go through jungle, lots of creepers, the 'pop-a-gun' tree and bearded fig clinging to the cliff (note the stalactites and stalagmites); a section devoted to palms and ferns: golden, silver, macarthur and cohune palms, nutmegs and wild chestnuts; to open areas with tall leafy mahogany trees, rock balsam and mango trees. At the end of the walk are ponds with lots of frogs and toads. Best of all though is the wonderful view to the coast. On the left are some steps leading to a gazebo, at the same level as the tops of the cabbage palms. Look out for monkeys at dawn and dusk.

Harrison's Cave

ⓘ *T417 3700, www.harrisonscave.com, tram tours daily 0845-1545, US$30.30, children US$15.15, 4-hr adventure tour 0900, 1200, through caves with knee pads and headlamps US$101.01, no children, book in advance.*

The Gully is connected geologically to nearby Harrison's Cave, just to the south. This little tourist trap has an impressive visitors' centre with restaurant (fair), shop and a small display of local geology and Amerindian artefacts. You are first shown an interesting video of Barbados' geology, then taken into the limestone cave on an electric 'train'. The visit takes about 30-40 minutes and you will see some superbly lit stalactites and stalagmites, waterfalls and large underground lakes. Be prepared to get a bit wet as the caves drip. There is a guide to point out the interesting formations and two stops for photo-opportunities.

If you take Highway 2 heading to Bridgetown you will pass **Jack-in-the-Box Gully**, part of the same complex of Welchman Hall Gully and Harrison's Cave. **Coles Cave**

Immigrants and settlers

There were Amerindians on Barbados for a thousand years or more. The first Europeans to find the island were the Portuguese, who named it 'Os Barbados' after the bearded fig trees which grew on the beaches, and left behind some wild pigs. These bred successfully and provided meat for the first English settlers, who arrived in 1627 and found an island which was otherwise uninhabited. It is not clear why the Amerindians abandoned Barbados, although several theories exist. King Charles I gave the Earl of Carlisle permission to colonize the island and it was his appointed Governor, Henry Hawley, who in 1639 founded the House of Assembly. Within a few years, there were over 40,000 white settlers, mostly small farmers, and equivalent in number to about 1% of the total population of England at this period. After the 'sugar revolution' of the 1650s most of the white population left. For the rest of the colonial period sugar was king, and the island was dominated by a small group of whites who owned the estates, the 'plantocracy'. The majority of the population today is descended from African slaves who were brought in to work on the plantations; but there is a substantial mixed-race population, and there has always been a small number of poor whites, particularly in the east part of the island. Many of these are descended from 100 prisoners transported in 1686 after the failed Monmouth rebellion and Judge Jeffrey's 'Bloody Assizes'.

(an 'undeveloped' cave nearby, which can easily be explored with a waterproof torch or flashlight) lies at its north end.

Flower Forest
① *Richmond Plantation, St Joseph, turn off Highway 2 on the Melvin Hill road just after the agricultural station and follow the signs. T433 8152, www.flowerforestbarbados.com, daily 0900-1700, US$12.50, 4-12s half price, café and toilets, good information sheet,*
North of Welchman Hall Gully is this 53.6-acre, landscaped former plantation, 270 m above sea level, opened in 1983 with beautifully laid out gardens. The original wooden plantation house, which used to house the snack bar unfortunately burned down in 1990, so the current administration building was built to replace it. Named paths wend their way around the hillside; they are well maintained and even suitable for wheelchairs, although there are a few which go off the beaten track and can only be negotiated on foot. The garden contains species not only from Barbados but also from all over the world, they are beautifully arranged with plenty of colour all year round. You can find heliconias, ginger lilies, orchids, anthurium, ixoras and bougainvillea as well as productive plants such as bananas, cocoa, coffee and breadfruit. The outstanding feature of this garden, however, is the forest. Enormous trees loom above you, with Royal and other palms giving shade to the paths, while in between you can find bearded fig trees, huge baobab and mango trees. Here and there they open onto large grassy areas affording excellent views over the valley to the east coast. Liv's Lookout in particular has a fantastic outlook all up the northeast seaboard. To the west you can see Mount Hillaby, at 340 m the island's highest point (see page 50 for walking from Farley Hill). The gardeners pride themselves on using only natural fertilizers and no herbicides, except on the orchids, where they use environmentally friendly products.

Springvale Eco-Heritage Museum

ⓘ *Highway 2, St Andrew, T438 7011, Mon-Sat 1000-1600, Sun by appointment, café.*

Springvale is an 80-ha former sugar plantation and the manager's house has been converted into a folk museum of Barbados with a presentation of historical rural Barbadian life. It is very low key and informal, and worth a detour if you are in the area. The owner, Newlands Greenidge, can trace his ancestry back to 1631 and a ship which came from Greenwich. He will explain the day-to-day items in the museum, showing how people used to live in colonial times, and will take you along a path outside pointing out the various plants and their uses. The café serves local juices and food according to what is in season.

Hunte's Gardens

ⓘ *T433 3333, www.huntesgardensbarbados.com, open daily, closed Jun, US$15.*

A short distance away along Highway 3A at Castle Grant is another treat for keen gardeners, Hunte's Gardens, which can easily be combined with visits to Orchid World, Flower Forest and Andromeda Gardens. Genial host, horticulturist Anthony Hunte, has lovingly created this rainforest garden in a gully, with flowering plants growing in a variety of habitats, from sunny, open spaces to a dark sink hole. A pretty path wends its way through a series of little gardens tucked away in private areas with strategically placed benches where you can pause to admire the view and watch the birds and butterflies. At the end you are welcomed back to the veranda of the house for a rum punch or fruit juice and an entertaining chat with the owner and his dog, Flora. Plants can be purchased from the nursery.

Speightstown

Speightstown, in the parish of St Peter, is the second largest town on the island, the major shopping destination and bus terminus in the north, but barely more than a village. It is a lively place during opening hours, but dead as a door nail the rest of the time. Pronounced Spikestown or Spikestong in broad dialect, it is named after William Speight, who once owned the land, a merchant and member of the Governor Hawley's first House of Assembly. Richard Ligon, who wrote a history of the island, published in 1657, referred to it as Spykeses Bay. An important port in the early days, when it was known as Little Bristol, because of its trade with Bristol, England; it also traded heavily with Bridgetown, 1½ hours' sailing time to the south for a schooner, and used to have four jetties. It also once had three forts, no longer in evidence: Orange Fort, Coconut Fort and Denmark Fort, while outside town were Dover Fort and Heywoods Battery. They didn't see a lot of action but the town was once invaded by Oliver Cromwell's forces when Barbados remained loyal to King Charles I. Colonel Alleyne led the Roundheads ashore in December 1651 only to be shot dead by Royalists. His forces captured the town, their only victory, and a peace treaty was later signed at Oistins.

Places in Speightstown

Speightstown has several interesting old buildings and many two-storey shops with Georgian balconies and overhanging galleries. Sadly many have been knocked down by passing lorries and a fire in 1941 destroyed almost everything near the bridge on the main road, Queen Street. On Queen Street, **Arlington House** is a 17th-century single house, ie a single room wide. It is believed to have been the prototype for the Charleston Single, common in Charleston, South Carolina, but is the last remaining example on Barbados.

The Hag

Among the folk legends of Barbados handed down through generations of slaves is one about evil spirits called 'hags', similar to witches. These were women, often those in authority such as planters' wives, who were believed to shed their skin at night and turn into a ball of fire in their search for blood. If the skin was found and rubbed with pepper and salt, the hag would not be able to put it back on and would die. The last person in Barbados thought to have been a hag died in the 1920s.

It tapers towards the back and the ground floor room was once believed to have been a chandlers, as the original owners, the Skinners, owned one of the jetties. There is a separate entrance to the first floor room and above that there is an attic with gabled windows. The house has been beautifully renovated and is now a state of the art interactive **museum** ① *T422 4064, see Facebook, Mon-Sat 0900-1700, US$12.50,* with tours and audio visual displays, including videos of interviews with members of the local community.

St Peter's Parish Church was first built of timber in 1629, but there was a second building in 1665 and then it was rebuilt in 1837 in early Georgian style. However, a fire in 1980 damaged the original east window, pulpit and font. It was restored in 1983, using the original walls. On the other side of the road beside the sea is a blue and white stage with wooden bench seating for outdoor events. The **jetty** was built in 1998 and if you walk to the end you get a tremendous view along the coast from the Arawak cement plant in the north, Port St Charles marina, the town and beaches to the south, with lovely changing colours of turquoise, dark aquamarine and purple (depending on the lenses in your sunglasses). The **Fisherman's Pub**, alongside the jetty, also has a great view of the sea and is a useful watering hole during a tour of the island.

The newest attraction in town is a **trompe l'oeil mural** depicting the history of Barbados in its many phases. Privately commissioned (by restauranteur Pierre Spenard) on the north wall of Jordan's supermarket warehouse on the seafront and officially unveiled in 2013, it measures 21 m by 7.5 m and was painted by John Pugh, of California, and Don Small, of Barbados. It is full of detail of the people and events that have created modern Barbados. It has been painted using the latest technology and materials to prevent weather damage and fading. Overlooking the sea, works have also created a new beach, complete with toilets and showers.

The National Trust oversees and maintains the award-winning **Arbib Nature & Heritage Trail** ① *reservations T234 9010/426 2421, walks Wed, Thu, Sat 0900-1400, US$25, minimum 4 people, or US$100,* walks with routes of 5.5 km and 7.5 km, starting from St Peter's church, Speightstown. Young local guides take small groups of hikers exploring side streets, cricket pitches, sugar plantations, forests and beaches. Older residents of the area have provided background information, with tales of the town's history, to spice up the guides' patter. You can choose from the Whim Adventure Tour of 3½ hours or the Round-de-Town Stroll of two hours. Well worth doing and even the adventure trail through Whim Gully is on relatively easy paths and roads.

Around Speightstown

Just south of Speightstown, accessed off Highway 1, is **Mullins Beach** a lovely stretch of beach with lots of activity, usually calm water and safe, roped off, area for snorkelling and

Beaches around Barbados

There are beaches along most of the south and west coasts. Although some hotels make it hard to cross their property to reach the sand, there are no private beaches in Barbados. The west coast beaches are very calm, and quite narrow, beach erosion is a serious worry. A swell can wash up lots of broken coral making it unpleasant underfoot. The south coast can be quite choppy, but there is more sand. The southeast, between the airport and East Point, has steep limestone cliffs with a series of small sandy coves with coconut trees, and waves which are big enough for surfing. **Bottom Bay** is currently *the* place to go. Be careful on the east side of the island, currents and undertow are strong in places. Don't swim where there are warning signs, or where there are no other bathers, even on a calm day. **Bathsheba**, on the east coast, is quite spectacular, with wonderful views. There are some nice beaches within easy reach of the capital, Bridgetown. **Paradise Beach** on the west coast north of Bridgetown is beautifully deserted. Go to north end of Spring Gardens Highway, then up west coast road Highway 1 for about half a mile, then turn sharp left. Drive down to Batts Rock Beach, walk south to get to Paradise Beach. You can keep going along the shoreline as far as Deepwater Harbour, a nice walk, mostly beach. Near the south end of this stretch is **Brandon's Beach** accessible also from Spring Gardens Highway, which can be crowded if there's a cruise ship in. Just south of Bridgetown is **Bayshore**, also set up as a beach facility for cruise passengers.

swimming. Jet skis and boats are kept further out, although they have to come to shore to moor. There are sunbeds and umbrellas for hire, US$10, and vendors will try and sell you watersports. There has been some erosion of the beach but it is still a lovely place to come for the day while the beach bar and restaurant has glorious views for sunset watching with a beer or cocktail.

A glitzy marina has been built at Heywoods Beach just north of Speightstown, known as **Port St Charles** ① *T419 1000, www.portstcharles.com*. It is a huge and impenetrable development with a massive wall around the outside to deter casual visitors, but is now an official port of entry into Barbados with coastguard, police and immigration on site for entry by yacht or helicopter. There are 145 residential units, restaurants, a yacht club, heliport and watersports as well as capacity for eight mega-yachts and 140 yachts. Water taxis scoot around the lagoon taking residents to the various facilities on site or on shopping trips further afield in Speightstown. Most of the apartments and villas are privately owned; some are available for short term holiday rental. Public access to the beach is between the marina and the (closed) Almond Beach Village, with a small road and parking.

North of Speightstown the road passes through the fishing villages of **Six Men's Bay**, **Little Good Harbour** and **Half Moon Fort**, where boat building is still done on the seashore. Fishing has always been an important activity in this area and Speightstown was even a whaling station until 1903.

North Coast → For listings, see pages 63-80.

The north of the island in the parish of St Lucy is mercifully free of buildings and unspoilt (apart from Arawak Cement Plant). It is at first green and lush around Stroud Point but becomes more desolate as you approach North Point. The northwest coast, being slightly sheltered from the Atlantic swells, has many sandy coves such as Archers Bay. The cliffs are quiet and easy to walk. You may spot turtles swimming in the sea. North Point, however, is a different story. The sea here can be rough and wild, the waves apparently unaware that Barbados is in their way, blocking their path across the Atlantic Ocean. Huge waves crash into eight miles of cliffs, creating tunnels, caves, platforms and enormous jacuzzis. Round the tip on the eastern side there are some lovely shingle coves to explore, favourite picnic spots but otherwise deserted. The northeastern part of the country is known as the Scotland District for its rugged appearance and similarities perceived by the first colonizers. Although the landscape doesn't match the majesty of the Scottish Highlands, it has its own charms and there are some fascinating places to explore.

Along the coast

Animal Flower Cave

① North Point, St Lucy, T439 8797, see Facebook, 0900-1600 daily, US$10, children US$5, bar decorated with business cars, flags and memorabilia, toilets, play area and souvenir shops outside.

One of the many caverns created by the pounding waves of the Atlantic Ocean is is this cave, with its mouth above the sea when it is calm. The 'animals' are sea anemones but there are now so few of them the cave should be renamed. There are various 'shapes' in the rock which are pointed out to you, some of them tinted by the oxidation of copper and iron, and a pool at the mouth of the cave where you can swim looking out to sea. The view from North Point over the cliffs and ledges is dramatic and well worth the trip even if (or particularly when) the cave is shut because of high seas. The main cave may be closed due to dangerous seas. The floor of the cave is very stony and can be slippery.

The Spout

Follow the rocky coast and turn into the abandoned North Point Surf Resort. Park outside the wall, the buildings are half ruined now, and there is an enormous empty swimming pool. From the dilapidated resort, you can walk around the Spout, which has lots of blow holes and a small, rather dangerous beach. Good walks along the cliffs can be enjoyed, for instance from River Bay to Little Bay along the Antilles Flat, but beware as there is no shade and there are shooting parties during the season. Several back roads go through the attractive communities of Spring Garden and St Clements. At Pie Corner you can rejoin the coast for Little Bay.

Little Bay

Little Bay is particularly impressive during the winter months with the swell breaking over the coral outcrops and lots of blowholes. Note the completely circular hole on the north edge of the Bay. If you climb through this natural archway in the cliff, there is a big, calm pool, just deep enough to swim between the cliffs and a line of rock on which the enormous waves break and send up a wall of spray. Wear shoes to stop your feet getting cut to pieces on the sharp rock.

Paul's Point

Paul's Point is a popular picnic area and very scenic. If the ground looks wet, park at the millwall by the Cove Stud Farm as it is easy to get bogged down. You get a good view of **Gay's Cove** below, with its shingle beach (safe to swim in the pools at low tide) and beyond it the 80-m-high Pico Teneriffe, a large rock (named by sailors who thought it looked like the mountain on Teneriffe in the Canaries) on top of a steeply sloping cliff. The white cliffs are oceanic rocks consisting of myriad tiny white shells or microscopic sea creatures. The whole of the coast to Bathsheba is visible and it is easy to see the erosion taking place in Corben's Bay. Indeed you get an excellent impression of the Scotland District, where the coral limestone has been eroded. The whole of this coast between North and Ragged Points has been zoned, no further development will be allowed along the seafront.

Jewish settlement

By the 1680s there were 300 Jews in Barbados, or 5% of the total population, and by the middle of the 18th century there were 800. They were heavily involved in the sugar industry, advancing capital and credit or owning plantations. The Morgan Stanley Mill was Jewish sugar and their influence was so great that Swan Street was once known as Jew Street. However, life was not a bed of roses for all of them. Jews were taxed more heavily than other residents and regularly expected to present the Governor with a 'Jew Pie', gold coins baked in a pie crust. They were not allowed to trade with blacks and were classed as 'foreigners and strangers'. In 1831 a storm destroyed the synagogue and the congregation began to decline, with emigration brought on by the end of slavery and the drop in the price of sugar. Enough Jews remained to rebuild the synagogue but by the turn of the 20th century only about 20 remained. In 1929 when only one man, Edmund Baeza, acknowledged his Jewish heritage, the synagogue was sold and in the 1950s was the office of the Barbados Turf Club. A small revival in the 1930s was brought about by the arrival in 1932 of a few Polish Jews fleeing Europe en route to Venezuela. They started working as peddlers and gradually attracted friends and other family members. Now there are Polish, Romanian, American, German, Guatemalan, Cuban and Chinese (converts) Jews and numbers fluctuate between 50 and 80.

After the French Revolution the threat of an invasion by France grew stronger. To increase their manpower, the British Army started to recruit black slaves. They were made free men and paid a wage, which attracted thousands to the Black Corps. By 1799 the corps became the West Indian Regiment, creating a formidable fighting force of 15,000 men.

Drax Hall, St George, was the first place on Barbados where sugar was cultivated in the 1640s and the 878-acre plantation is the only estate to have remained in the hands of the same family since the 17th century. The Great House vies with St Nicholas Abbey as the oldest plantation house on the island, both built in the 1650s.

Heading inland

Mount Gay Rum Distillery

North of the road between the St Lucy church junction and Alexandra, is the Mount Gay Rum Distillery. Rum distilled here is then shipped to Bridgetown where they have a Visitors' Centre, for blending, ageing and bottling. The distillery has been making rum since the 19th century and produces 500,000 gallons a year. There is no retail outlet here, it is a factory, plain and simple.

St Nicholas Abbey

ⓘ *Cherry Tree Hill, St Peter, T422 5357, www.stnicholasabbey.com, Sun-Fri 1000-1530, US$17.50, children US$10.*

Approached down a long and impressive avenue of mahogany trees and dating from around 1650 is this Abbey, one of the oldest domestic buildings in the English-speaking Americas (**Drax Hall** ⓘ *St George, open occasionally under the National Trust Open House programme*, is probably even older). Three storied, it has a façade with three ogee-shaped gables. It was never an abbey, some have supposed that the 'St' and 'Abbey' were added to impress, there being lots of 'Halls' in the south of the island. It is thought to have been built by Colonel Benjamin Beringer, but was sold to Sir John Yeamans, who set out from Speightstown in 1663 to colonize South Carolina. It is full of antiques, including an 1810 Coalport dinner service and a collection of early Wedgwood portrait medallions. Visitors are given an interesting tour of the ground floor of the house, the rum and sugar museum, gardens and the rum distillery. There is a 19th-century steam mill which operates several days a week. You can also watch a home movie showing life on a sugar plantation in the 1930s. It is narrated by Stephen Cave, the previous owner and son of the film maker. You will see the millwall in action and the many skilled workers from wheel wrights to coopers who made the plantation work. The importance of wind is emphasized. If the windmill stopped the whole harvest came to a halt as the cane which had been cut would quickly dry out if it was not crushed straight away. The waste was used to fuel the boilers just as it is today in sugar factories. Visitors are offered a complimentary drink and there is a pleasant café for lunch and tea behind the house near the 400-year-old sandbox tree. St Nicholas Abbey rum is sold locally only here at the shop, where they also sell gourmet sugars, jams, jellies and other sweet treats. From Cherry Tree Hill there are glorious views all over the Scotland District.

Morgan Lewis Sugar Mill
① St Peter, T422 7429.
At the bottom of the steep mahogany-lined Cherry Tree Hill you come to the National Trust-owned mill. A millwall with original machinery which the National Trust restored over a period of four years. Built around 1776 by Dutchmen, it is the largest, complete windmill in the Caribbean, with its wheel house and sails in working order. After completion of the renovation works it started to grind cane again in 1999 after a gap of 54 years. However, it was struck by lightening in 2007 and still under repair. The interpretative centre is not open but you can climb up into the mill and see the machinery. Note the 33-m tail, this enabled the operators to position the apparatus to maximize the effect of the wind. It is on a working farm. On the flat savannah at the bottom of the hill is a cricket pitch, a pleasant place to watch the game at weekends.

Grenade Hall Forest and Signal Station and Barbados Wildlife Reserve
① Highway 2, St Andrew, T422 8826, daily 1000-1700, US$11.75, 3-12s half price, café and shop, toilets, bus from Bridgetown, Holetown, Speightstown or Bathsheba.
This is a complex of attractions with something for all the family: animals, history, nature, and can easily absorb half a day during a tour of the north. The **Barbados Wildlife Reserve**, established with Canadian help in 1985, is set in four acres of mature mahogany off Highway 2. They have a huge collection of the large red-footed Barbados tortoise, apparently the largest in the world, which roam slowly around all over the paths, while brocket deer and agouti lounge about in the shade to escape the midday heat. Most of the animals are not caged, and you are warned to be careful as you wander around the paths through the trees. There is an architecturally interesting bird house with snakes upstairs and you look down through the floor to the aviary. The population of the rabbit pen is seriously out of control and the lone wallaby kept with the rabbits and guinea pigs looks stunned. It is a good place to see lots of Barbados green vervet monkeys close up if they haven't taken off to the forest next door. Do not touch them and do not eat food near them as they can get aggressive. The primate research centre helps to provide farmers

Monkeys and medicine

The **Barbados Primate Research Centre** at the Wildlife Reserve not only helps farmers to control numbers of green monkeys, which destroy crops, it also provides monkeys to zoos overseas and to laboratories for research. Many monkeys end up with pharmaceutical companies or medical research labs. Green monkey cells are used to manufacture the Sabin Polio Vaccine; one green monkey can provide up to 2.5 million doses and the Primate Research Centre is responsible for 70% of the world's polio vaccine.

with advice on how to control the green monkeys which were brought from Africa by the first settlers but now are regarded as a pest. The animals are fed near it at 1400. The centre has also developed a nature trail in the neighbouring Grenade Hall Forest, with over a mile of coral pathways and interpretative signs. They can be rough, steep and slippery and are definitely not wheelchair friendly. Try to be quiet, so as not to disturb birds and animals – a tricky job for kids.

An early 19th-century **signal station** is next to Grenade Hall Forest. It was one of six erected at strategic points on the island to relay messages from Bridgetown to the north in a matter of minutes by using flags or semaphores, but it closed in 1884, rendered obsolete by the telephone. It has now been restored and an audio tape gives the history with sound effects. There are a few archaeological exhibits and photos of the rebuilding work in 1991-1993. The wonderful panoramic view gives you a good idea of its original role in the communications network.

Farley Hill House

ⓘ Highway 2, St Peter, T422 3555, www.nccbarbados.gov.bb/farley-hill-park, daily 0830-1800, US$1.75, picnic tables, toilets.

On the other side of the road from the Wildlife Reserve, set in a pleasant park opened by the Queen in 1966, is the atmospheric ruin of Farley Hill House. The views over the Scotland District, right down to the light house on Ragged Point, are spectacular. A 19th-century plantation house damaged by fire, it was purchased by the Government in 1965 and declared a national park. Benches have been set at strategic points so you can just sit and gaze into the deep blue yonder and enjoy the breeze coming in off the Atlantic. There is a large number of imported and native tree species, some labelled, planted over 17 acres of woodland. There are picnic benches under the trees and it is popular with Bajan families on Sunday. You are recommended to go with a very serious picnic if you are planning to join them. It is also the venue for the annual Jazz Festival in January and Reggae on the Hill during Crop Over. It was once used as the location for the film, Island in the Sun, but it was after renovations for the movie that the house burned down. From Farley Hill it is possible to walk more or less along the top of the island as far as Mount Hillaby, through woods and then canefields. However, it helps to know where you are going as the paths have a mind of their own and losing them can be uncomfortable. You will see plenty of monkeys on the way and good views.

East Coast → *For listings, see pages 63-80.*

Wild and windy, unspoilt and untamed, the Atlantic coast has a raw energy and is stunningly beautiful. Craggy cliffs form a backdrop for huge bays filled with boulders which appear to have rolled down the hillsides into the foaming surf. This is not the place for safe swimming, Bajans say "the sea ain't got no back door", but it is the nearest place to heaven for surfers, who can be seen out there at any time of day waiting for the right wave. Hiking is also excellent, particularly along the abandoned railway track which hugs the coastline, and other outdoor activities such as horse riding or cycling. Bathsheba is the main village, where accommodation can be found, but otherwise the east coast is sparsely inhabited, dotted with colourful chattel houses enjoying a breezy sea view.

Inland, but within easy reach of either the east or west coast, are several stunning gardens and natural attractions such as ancient forests and caves.

Along the coast

The five-mile East Coast Road, opened by Queen Elizabeth II on 15 February 1966, runs from Belleplaine, where the railway ended, skirts Walker's Savannah and runs south to Long Pond, through Cattlewash, so named because Bajans brought their animals here to wash them in the sea, down to Bathsheba and on to Codrington College. The road affords fine views of meadows and palm trees tumbling into the ocean. Look out for grazing black-bellied sheep which are commonly mistaken for goats.

Barclays Park
ⓘ *Benab, St Andrew, north of Bathsheba, car parking, bus from Bathsheba or Speightstown, beach bar, T422 9213.*

Barclays Park is a large open space and a good place to stop for a picnic under the shady casuarina trees. It is the venue for the Party Monarch calypso competition during Crop Over. The 50-acre park was given to the government of Barbados by Barclays Bank to commemorate independence in 1966. Walk up Chalky Mount for magnificent views of the east coast, easily reached at the end of the bus line from Bridgetown. If you ask locally for the exact path you are likely to be given several different routes. Some people say that the Mount looks like the figure of a man resting with his hands over his stomach and it is known locally as 'Napoleon'. While up here you can visit the Chalky Mount Potteries in the village, where they use a potter's wheel of a design that is hundreds of years old. You can see them at work and buy their produce. Walk down through the meadows to Barclays Park for a drink when you come down. Staff in the café will know times of buses to either Bathsheba or Speightstown. The East Coast Road continues a little further north to Long Pond, then skirts Walker's Savannah to Belleplaine, where the railway ended.

Turners Hall Woods
Inland and west of Barclays Park and Chalky Mount and reached from St Simon's Church are Turners Hall Woods, a good vantage point. It is thought that the wood has changed little to that which covered the island before the English arrived, although it is less specialized than a true tropical forest, with only 13 species of lianas and three species of epiphyte. The 50-acre patch of tropical mesophytic forest has never been clear-felled (although individual trees were often taken out) and it managed to survive the massive clearance for sugar cane which took place in the 17th century. You can walk over the steep paths here and see many species, ranging from the sandbox tree to the 100-ft locust trees supported by massive buttresses. This is the only place where you can see Jack-in-the-box trees on Barbados and the forest is a sanctuary for them. The island's first natural gas field was here and the main path through the wood is the remains of the old road.

Cattlewash to St Martin's Bay
A sandy beach stretches for miles along the sweeping curve of the coast line from Cattlewash to St Martin's Bay and there are many spots where you can sit and sunbathe, admire the view and do a bit of beachcombing for whatever may have come over from Africa. The tiny hamlet of **Bathsheba** has a double bay with wave-eroded rocks and boulders at each end and in the middle. The beach is sandy but at the water's edge it turns to flat rocks, platforms interspersed with rock pools where you can cool off at low tide. Windswept and with pounding surf, swimmers confine themselves to these pools, best in the shelter of the enormous boulders (watch out for sea urchins), but Bathsheba is the place for surfing

East coast railway line

A railway was built in 1883 (but closed in 1937) between Bridgetown and Bathsheba. Originally conceived as going to Speightstown, it actually went up the east coast to a terminus at Belleplaine, St Andrew. The cutting at My Lady's Hole, near Conset Bay in St John is spectacular, with a gradient of 1:31, which is supposed to have been the steepest in the world except for rack and pinion and other special types of line. The railway here suffered from landslides, wave erosion, mismanagment and underfunding so that the 37-mile track was in places in very bad condition. The crew would sprinkle sand on the track, the first-class passengers remained seated, the second-class walked and the third-class pushed. There is good walking along the old railway track.

The section from Bathsheba through Bath to Consett Bay is mostly in good condition, although you have to scramble on some bits. It takes about 1½ hours from Bathsheba to Bath, where most people stop to cool off in the sea. South of Consett, there used to be a railway station and sugar factory at Three Houses. The area has now been landscaped and made into a new picnic area, called Three Houses Park.

and the bay seems to be almost white as the surf trails out behind the Atlantic rollers. The popular surf spots are Soup Bowl and Parlour, where waves break consistently year round but are best between September and November. Surfing championships are often held here. Low key accommodation is available in Bathsheba, the only place on the coast where you can find anywhere to stay, and there are a few places to eat. **Hackleton's Cliff**, which runs parallel with the coast just inland from Bathsheba, was allegedly named after a man called Hackleton who committed suicide by riding his horse over the cliff.

Perched up on the hillside with a fabulous view of the ocean are the **Andromeda Gardens** ① *Bathsheba, St Joseph, T433 9384, daily 0900-1700, US$10, 6-12s US$5*, one of Barbados' foremost gardens, above the bay at Hillcrest, within walking distance of the beach but uphill all the way – hot work. Now owned by the Barbados National Trust, it is leased to Caribbean Horticultural Services and the University of the West Indies has responsibility for research and educational activities here. The gardens contain plants from all over Barbados as well as species from other parts of the world, particularly Asia, amounting to over 600 species in total. They were collected by the late Iris Bannochie, who started laying out the garden trails in 1954 alongside a stream, now a prominent water feature. In 1988 she willed the gardens to the National Trust so that they would be open to the public in perpetuity. There are many varieties of orchid, heliconia, hibiscus and flowering trees and its blooms are regular winners at the Chelsea Flower Show in London. You have a choice of two walks through immaculate gardens, sprawling over the hillside between limestone boulders. It is always full of interest and colour, with good explanatory leaflets for each walk, telling you of the uses of each plant as well as where to stop and rest. The Hibiscus Café has good juices, closes 1645 in time for staff to catch the 1700 bus back to Bridgetown. For lovers of gardens, two others within reach of Bathsheba are the **Flower Forest**, see page 42 and **Orchid World**, see page 34.

Bath

Southeast of Bathsheba with access off the East Coast Road, just east of the Satellite Earth Station, is the very pleasant beach and picnic spot at Bath. There are a few beach villas at one end, but otherwise this is an empty, unspoilt beach with a long sweep of casuarina trees for shade. The sand is good but at high tide the sea covers it completely and you have to retreat into the trees. Low tide is wonderful with rock pools to wallow in for a lovely lazy day. Swimming is reasonably safe here because of an offshore reef, but you have to be careful of the rocks. Popular with Bajans at weekends, when families pitch camp around a picnic table, it is deserted during the week and highly recommended for escaping the crowds. The beach bar usually offers a dish of the day for lunch, often fish fry, or you can get a flying fish sandwich, chips, chicken wings or fish cakes to fill a nagging hole. Not only is there a children's playground, there is also a large grass area for games such as football or cricket, where young men work off their surplus energy and kids practice their bowling and batting skills.

St John's Church

Inland, on the other side of the East Coast Road, is St John's Church, Pothouse, Parish Church of St John. Perched high up on an 800-ft cliff with views over the Scotland District and the entire rugged east coast, St John's was first built in 1660. However, it was a victim of the great hurricane of 1835 and had to be rebuilt. There is an interesting pulpit made from six different kinds of wood. You will also find the grave of Fernando Paleologus "descendant of ye imperial line of ye last Christian emperors of Greece". The full story is in Patrick Leigh Fermor's The Traveller's Tree. There are some fine Royal palms in the churchyard, also known as Cabbage palms (roystonea oleracea), and it is interesting to stroll around but pick your moment. The church is on the itinerary for island tours and you may be jostling for space with the occupants of the latest cruise ship in port.

Codrington College

ⓘ www.codrington.org.

Also in this area is Codrington College, one of the most famous landmarks on the island which can be seen from the East Coast Road down an avenue of Cabbage (Royal) palm trees. It is steeped in history as the first Codrington landed in Barbados in 1628. His son acted as Governor for three years but was dismissed for liberal views. Instead he stood for parliament and was elected speaker for nine years. He was involved in several wars against the French and became probably the wealthiest man in the West Indies. The third Codrington succeeded his father as Governor-General of the Leeward islands, attempted to stamp out the considerable corruption of the time and distinguished himself in campaigns (especially in taking St Kitts). He died in 1710, a bachelor aged 42, and left his Barbadian properties to the Society for the Propagation of the Gospel in Foreign Parts. It was not until 1830 that Codrington College, where candidates could study for the Anglican priesthood, was established. From 1875 to 1955 it was associated with Durham University, England. Apart from its beautiful grounds with huge lily pond (flowers close up in the middle of the day) and impressive façade, there is a chapel containing a plaque to Sir Christopher Codrington and a library. Visitors are welcome to stroll around the gardens, where there is a beautiful lily pond (the flowers close up in the middle of the day) stocked with fish and ducks, and there are even picnic benches and a playground, with a wonderful view of the Atlantic coast behind the college. You can follow the track which drops down 120 metres to the sea at the beautiful Conset Bay. Visitors are also welcome to join services of worship in the chapel, where donations are appreciated.

Ragged Point

The automatic East Point lighthouse on Ragged Point on the most easterly point of the island stands among the ruined houses of the former lighthouse keepers. There are good views north towards Conset Point, the small Culpepper island, and the south coast. Note the erosion to the 27-m cliffs caused by the Atlantic sweeping into the coves. An atmospheric station close to the shoreline measures air quality; this is the first landfall after blowing across the Atlantic from the coast of Africa.

South Coast → *For listings, see pages 63-80.*

The south coast caters for the package holiday end of the market, with lots of mid-range, mid-quality hotels packed in along the western end in districts with the charming English names of Hastings, Worthing and Dover. There is little to distinguish them nowadays as the coast is entirely built up from Hastings to Oistins, but St Lawrence Gap, known as just The Gap, is the place to go for nightlife and Maxwell is the base for the Barbados Windsurfing Club. The advantage of the south coast is that it is close to the airport, has the better beaches, with wider expanses of sand and gently sloping entry to the sea. It is popular with a younger crowd and there is lots of night time action. Families with young children and teenagers find plenty to do, day and night, and it is easy to get round the island for excursions when you've had enough of the beach. Shopping is good if you are self-catering, there are lots of different restaurants and bars, sports bars and gift shops. Tucked away behind the hotel strip is the Graeme Hall Nature Sanctuary, where you can go for a change of scenery and a bit of birdwatching. Oistins, a fishing village, sparks into life on Friday nights for a fish fry and the Crane is a magnet for lovers of Sunday brunch and steel bands. The south coast is great for windsurfing and kitesurfing, particularly to the east of South Point, where Silver Sands is a windsurfer's Mecca, but watch out for rip tides if you are swimming.

Beaches to the east of Six Cross Roads

Six Cross Roads (Six Roads since a roundabout was installed to sort out traffic accidents) is the main junction and point of reference in the southeast. For the beaches in this area, from here take Highway 5 heading northeast. After the turning for Sam Lord's Castle look out for a small signpost on a telegraph pole for Bottom Bay. Go down a small road through grazing cattle to the parking place near Bottom Bay House.

Bottom Bay

This just has to be the most beautiful beach in Barbados and one of the best in the Caribbean. What is more, it is often deserted, even in high season, but even with a few couples on the beach you will feel as though you've got the place to yourselves. Steep cliffs surround the small bay and the sand is a glorious pale coral pink. Walk down steps carved between the cliffs onto a huge expanse of sand, where a clump of palm trees grows in true holiday brochure fashion. Sometimes there is a boy on the beach who will offer to climb up to get coconuts down for you to drink the cool milk. He will ask for an extortionate tip for his labour, but the coconuts are free. There is a little hut under the coconut palms where you can sometimes hire sun beds, but it is not always open, even in high season. The only shade is under the palm trees or the cliffs, but with few other people around, that is usually plenty. The sea is often rough with quite big waves, better for jumping and splashing about than swimming.

Before you leave, go up on top of the cliffs to look back down onto the beach, then walk round to get a good view of the next bay south, **Cove Bay**, with the ruins of Harrismith plantation house overlooking the water, yet to be renovated and developed. The beach, also sometimes called **Harrismith Beach**, has no facilities. The strip of sand is narrower than that at Bottom Bay and palm trees grow behind the beach, but there is a lagoon formed by a reef, which gives protection for bathers.

Long Bay

The next beach is on Long Bay, a glorious stretch of pink sand that was once used by guests at the hotel, **Sam Lord's Castle**. Samuel Hall Lord (1778-1844) reputedly hung lanterns in the trees to look like the mouth of Carlisle Harbour and lure ships onto Cobbler's Reef where they were shipwrecked. There is supposed to be a tunnel from the beach to the castle's cellars to facilitate his operation. The proceeds made him a wealthy man although the 'castle', a regency building built in 1820, was probably financed from his marriage to a wealthy heiress who later left him and fled to England. Another legend has it that the captain of one of the wrecked ships murdered Sam Lord in London in 1844. Wander down to the cove where there is a good example of a turtlecrawl, a salt water pond enclosed by a wall. Here turtles were kept alive until wanted for the kitchen. The castle was converted to a luxury hotel in the 20th century, attracting royalty and film stars, but it gradually declined until it was abandoned at the start of the 21st century. Despite a buy-out and plans for redevelopment, nothing happened. In 2010 a mysterious fire gutted the once-magnificent building and only the shell now remains. However, you can walk through the grounds to gain access to the beach, which is magnificent.

Crane Beach

Crane Beach is another fabulously deep beach with plenty of powder soft coral pink sand, while the water is a picture-book turquoise. The waves are a bit rough for swimming but very popular with body surfers and great for splashing about and generally having fun. At certain times of the year the beach is covered in seaweed, which is unpleasant. There is a luxury hotel with condos perched on top of cliffs at the southern end of the beach and these provide natural shade if you don't want to hire an umbrella. There was once a crane on the top for loading and unloading ships, hence the name. A rickety path winds part of the way around the cliffs, a useful vantage point from which boys drop fishing lines into the water, but the sea has eroded the rocks so that the cliff now overhangs the waves and the end of the path has collapsed. Sunday is the popular day here, when the Crane Hotel lays on a huge buffet lunch to the accompaniment of steel pan. They will even hire you clothes so you can look decent when you come off the beach to eat in the restaurant, which has an eagle's eye view of the bay. The hotel opened in 1867, making it the oldest hotel on the island, although the original building dates from the 18th century. The more recent construction of timeshare apartments mars the skyline but they are invisible from the beach. You can either park by the hotel or carry on to a little roundabout by Crane House and turn down a narrow lane which leads to steps giving access to the northern end of the beach. Parking is not good here and extremely difficult on a Sunday. You may have to reverse out. If you park at the hotel they will charge you access through their grounds to the beach, redeemable against a drink at the bar, but at least you can use their toilets. Sunbeds, umbrellas and boogie boards for hire on the beach

Foul Bay

Just south of Crane Beach, on the other side of the hotel, is Foul Bay, which has no facilities. Take the turning signed 'Public Access to Foul Bay Beach'. Another long stretch of idyllic pink sand with turquoise water, wide and open and less crowded than at the Crane although conditions in the sea are similar. This is the longest beach on this coast, with large cliffs at each end. There is some shade and a few picnic tables and benches, so ideal if you want to be self-sufficient and take your own food and drink. A small fishing fleet comes ashore here and you can sometimes see turtles just beyond the waves.

Sunbury Plantation House

ⓘ *Turn north on Highway 4B at Six Roads roundabout, the plantation house is at the 1st T-junction, T423 6270, www.barbadosgreathouse.com, daily 0930-1700, last tour at 1630, US$10, restaurant in the courtyard.*

This is one of the oldest houses on the island and a fascinating insight into plantation life. Sunbury (pronounced Sun-berry) was built around 1660 from local rocks and ballast brought over in the ships from England, held together with a durable cement of limestone, sand, crushed coral and egg white. Originally it had a fishpond roof for collecting water but this was damaged in the 1780 hurricane and was replaced in 1788. The Chapman family who built the house were among the first settlers and related to the Earl of Carlisle (see box, page 42), who granted them land. Chapmans are mentioned on the first map of the island in 1938 and again in Richard Ford's map of 1674 which shows a cattle mill on the Chapman plantation. It changed hands and names several times, owned by the Brankers, Butler Harris and the Barrow family (who named it Sunbury after their home in England). One of the Barrow heirs was Colonel in Charge during the Easter Rebellion of 1816, see box, page 59, during which the plantation suffered damage valued at £4000. The slave revolt at Sunbury was led by a friend of Bussa called King William, who was later put to death. The estate never really recovered and in 1835 John Barrow sold up and emigrated to Newfoundland. The new owners, the Daniels, had made their money out of shipping

The Easter Rebellion

The 1816 Easter Rebellion was an uprising by slaves who thought (incorrectly) that William Wilberforce had introduced a bill in the English parliament granting slaves their freedom. It was thought by the slaves that the Barbados plantation owners were denying them this freedom. Despite destroying a large acreage of cane fields, no owners or their families were killed and the uprising was quickly crushed by the West Indian Regiment. Several hundred slaves were killed in battle or hanged afterwards, including the best-known leader, an African called Bussa, and Washington Francklyn, a free man of mixed race who was thought, probably erroneously, to have planned the rebellion. 123 slaves were exiled to Sierra Leone.

sugar to England and owned several sugar estates but were absentee landlords. At the end of the 19th century, a Scotsman, Alistair Cameron, emigrated to Barbados, married a niece of the Barrows and in 1896 bought the Estates of Sunbury, Hampton and Bushy Park after the death of Thomas Daniel. Two of the Cameron daughters remained living at Sunbury until their deaths in 1980 and 1981, when the land was sold to the estate manager and the house was sold to Angela and Keith Melville. They took on a house which had been untouched for 100 years, and although they lived in it for a few years, in 1984 they moved back to their previous house and opened the whole of Sunbury House as a museum. In 1995 a fire swept through the upper floors destroying the old timbers, wooden floors and antiques, except for those in the cellar. Substantial renovation was needed but the massive walls and a few floorboards were intact. The house/museum is now crammed with a very busy collection of mahogany furniture, art, china and antiques found elsewhere on the island or returned to Barbados from abroad. You can roam all over it as, unusually, there is access to the upstairs rooms. In the cellars, you can see the domestic quarters with a good collection of old optical instruments and household items. In the cellar and in the garden there are lots of carts and gigs, including one donated by Sir Harry Llewellyn, the British Olympic showjumper of the 1950s and 1960s.

Foursquare Rum Factory and Heritage Park

ⓘ *Foursquare, St Philip, T420 9954/420 1977, Mon-Fri 0900-1700, Sat 1000-2100, Sun 1200-1800.*

This is the most modern rum distillery in Barbados, if not the world, on the site of an old sugar factory dating back to 1636. They make several rums here, including ESA Field White Rum and also specializing in spiced rum. You get a very interesting, free, tour of the distillery to see all the manufacturing processes, then an informative tasting session of their rums, which are available to buy, although there is little sales pressure. The Heritage Park comprises the old sugar buildings, with sugar machinery, craft market, pottery, bottling plant, folk museum, pet farm, pony stables and Foundry Art Gallery, not all of which are open at any one time.

The southeast coast

Enterprise

West of the airport, off Highway 7 just east of Oistins, is **Miami Beach**, also known as **Enterprise**. This is a good and popular beach in two parts, calm or rougher, so suitable for small children or older, braver types. Swimming is good, but don't go far out. The general rule everywhere is stay within your depth. There is a life guard. Windsurfing is popular, particularly for those at an intermediate level. There is lots of shade under casuarina and broadleaf trees and everything you could need for a pleasant day on the beach, including beach chair and umbrella rental, toilets, picnic tables and a snack van. Catamaran tour parties often anchor here for lunch if the west coast is too rough for them to go up to see the turtles at Alleynes Bay. Cars park on the sand in the shade of the trees.

Oistins

Oistins, the main town in the parish of Christ Church, was named after Edward Oistine, a plantation owner in the area. It was important in colonial times as one of the sites where Roundheads and Cavaliers clashed, with the Royalists achieving a stand-off for six months. On 11 January 1652 a meeting took place in Ye Mermaid Tavern in Oistins, when the Articles of Agreement were signed. This later became known as the Charter of Barbados when recognized by the Commonwealth Parliament. Christ Church parish church overlooks the town and is notable for its cemetery containing the Chase Vault. When the vault was opened in 1812 for the burial of Colonel Thomas Chase, the lead coffins were found scattered around inside. It happened again in 1816, 1817, 1819 and 1820, whereupon the coffins were removed and buried separately in the churchyard. Whatever had been moving them around had thrown them about with such violence that one coffin had taken a chunk out of the vault wall.

Oistins is now the main fishing port with colourful boats pulled up on the shore and you can still see fishermen mending and making nets. The fish market is worth visiting, even if you don't want to buy, to see the expert skill and lightening speed with which the women fillet flying fish and bag them up for sale. Flying fish being the signature dish of Barbados, they make it into something special here, celebrating every Friday night with a fish fry around the market. Dozens of wooden stalls are opened for the occasion and the smell of well-seasoned fried fish wafts along the coast attracting hundreds of hungry people keen to fill up before hitting the bars and night spots of the south coast. Oistins is also the venue for an Easter Fish Festival, see page 14, celebrating fishermen's skills with demonstrations of fish boning, boat racing and crab racing, helped along with steel pan music and dancing.

Dover Beach and Sandy Beach

Between Maxwell and St Lawrence Gap is this beautiful horse shoe shaped bay with pristine white sand and turquoise water, picture book stuff. It is a great place for lazing around, sunbathing and cooling off in the sea, which is usually calm and protected. This is the main area for nightlife, with many restaurants, bars and clubs, some of which are in idyllic locations overlooking the water.

Further along the coast, **Sandy Beach**, Worthing, is also known as Carib Beach. The curve of the coastline and an offshore reef has produced a lovely beach with shallow, calm water, almost in a lagoon, making it ideal for families with small children. It is also a good place to learn to windsurf because of the lack of waves. The Carib Beach Bar attracts all

People

Barbados has a population of 284,000. This is more than any of the Windwards or Leewards, and is considered enough to make the island one of the 'big four' in the Caribbean Community. With population density of 655 per sq km in 2011, Barbados is one of the most crowded countries in the world.

Because Barbados lies upwind from the main island arc, it was hard to attack from the sea, so it never changed hands in the colonial wars of the 17th and 18th centuries. There is no French, Dutch, or Spanish influence to speak of in the language, cooking or culture. People from other islands have often referred to Barbados as Little England, and have not always intended a compliment. Today, the more obvious outside influences on the Barbadian way of life are North American. Most contemporary Barbadians stress their Afro-Caribbean heritage and aspects of the culture which are distinctively 'Bajan'. There are extremes of poverty and wealth, but these are not nearly so noticeable as elsewhere in the Caribbean. This makes the social atmosphere relatively relaxed. However, there is a history of deep racial division. Although there is a very substantial black middle class and the social situation has changed radically since the 1940s and 50s, there is still more racial intolerance on all sides than is apparent at first glance. Barbadians are a religious people and although the main church is Anglican, there are over 140 different faiths and sects, including Baptists, Christian Scientists, Jews, Methodists, Moravians and Roman Catholics.

sorts and is lively during the day and into the night. Park at Sandy Beach Resort or the Carib Beach Bar. Beach chairs, umbrellas and towels for hire.

Graeme Hall Nature Sanctuary

① *Worthing, Christ Church, Highway 7, T435 9727, www.graemehall.com, Mon-Fri 0730-1700, Sat 0800-1630, Sun 0900-1630.*

This is the largest expanse of inland water in Barbados, and the largest green space on the south coast, with a total of 240 acres. Some 35 acres are a sanctuary and 81 acres of wetland and mangroves around a lake have been designated as a RAMSAR site, a wetland of international importance recognized by the Convention on Wetlands Treaty. However, it is under threat from pollution and government inactivity. The ecosystem has become essentially a freshwater system rather than a brackish estuarine system. Seawater is unable to enter the wetland because of a broken government sluice gate that controls drainage and tidal seawater charges, and because government-sanctioned development has closed off other traditional sea-to-wetland waterways. As a result, freshwater drainage is now overwhelming the wetland, and while Barbados' most significant mangrove woodland can indeed survive in fresh water, any open area in the mangrove system caused by catastrophic hurricane, fire or disease will mean that the mangrove will not grow back. Despite a well-supported petition for the 240-acre wetland and upland buffer area to become a National Park, the government has included much of it in the zone for commercial and residential development. It is a natural habitat for birds and there are 18 resident species and some 150 migrants. Some 180 bird species have been recorded in Barbados, mostly migrants and mainly shore birds and waders, which breed in North America and winter in South America. The first to pass through are normally sighted in

July when they flock into the swamp. Three endangered Caribbean duck species are found here and there are also more familiar flamingos and parrots around the ponds. The swamp was saved from development by a retired Canadian, Peter Allard, who bought it in 1994. A café and lawn at the lakeside are open to the public but the rest is a bird sanctuary for scientific research only.

Accra Beach, in Rockley (and often referred to as Rockley Beach), off Highway 7, is in the middle of the hotel strip and is understandably popular and often crowded. It has a life guard, car park, kiosks for vendors, and beach chairs and boogie boards can be hired. Strong swimmers should head out to a small, man-made reef of huge boulders for the best snorkelling on the south coast. Sunk in the late 1990s, it is already growing coral and is home to large schools of blue tang, jacks and other colourful fish. A hawksbill turtle sometimes hangs around there and you may be lucky enough to see him if not too many boatloads of snorkellers have been there first. You must be careful on such a young reef not to damage anything by standing on it or poking around with your hands. Coral dies if you touch it. Depending on the waves, Accra Beach is also good for body surfing or, alternatively, just sitting watching the fit types performing and strutting their stuff. Despite controversy and environmental concerns, a **boardwalk** has been built along the coast from here to Hastings, about 1.5 km, which makes a pleasant stroll or a good early morning jog. Its construction has led to changes in the coastline resulting in the expansion of some beaches and the creation of other sandy areas. There are police patrols but take care if walking along it at night as it is unlit. There are a number of bars and restaurants along the route and places to sit and watch the world go by. It is so close to the sand that high tides bring piles of sand onto the boardwalk, but this is soon shovelled off. It is also close enough to see nesting and hatching turtles, while you might need to watch out for crabs sometimes.

Barbados listings

For hotel and restaurant price codes and other relevant information, see pages 10-13.

🛏 Where to stay

Bridgetown: Garrison Historic Area
p29

$$$$ Savannah Beach, Hastings, between Garrison Savannah and beach, T434 3800, www.savannahbarbados.com. All-inclusive. 92 rooms and suites, some in renovated historic building, mahogany furniture, wrought iron balconies, each room different, the rest in new blocks in similar design, rooms nearest beach can be noisy because of entertainment at beach bar, high-quality facilities, friendly service, gym, pool meanders through property. The hotel meets the sea at a coral outcrop, but you can walk down either side to a soft sand beach.

West Coast *p35, map p38*

$$$$ Cobblers Cove, just south of Speightstown, St Peter, T422 2291, www.cobblerscove.com. Small and exclusive, English country-house style suites, very comfortable, member of Relais & Chateaux, excellent service, high proportion of repeat business. The beach is narrow but guests tend to lounge around the kidney-shaped pool instead or head for the watersports area to the side, where there is more sand. Elegant restaurant with dress code.

$$$$ Coral Reef Club, Holetown, St James, T422 2372, www.coralreefbarbados.com. Lovely landscaped gardens with 12 acres of grounds, lawn running down to sea, cottages and villas in plantation style, very highly regarded, a Small, Luxury Hotel of the World. Elegant dining with weekly specials and evening entertainment

$$$$ The House, Paynes Bay, T432 5525, www.thehousebarbados.com. The height of luxury where your personal 'ambassador' brings cold towels and drinks to your sunbed and you get a jet lag revival massage

on arrival. 34 suites around a courtyard, beautifully decorated and furnished with lots of facilities, **Daphne's** restaurant alongside, breakfast, tea and canapés included. Well regarded for service and atmosphere, which is unpretentious. Use of facilities of **Tamarind Cove** next door and **Colony Club**, sister properties and part of Elegant Hotels.

$$$$ Little Good Harbour, north of Speightstown, T439 3000, www.littlegood harbourbarbados.com. Small wooden villas around pool, across the road from the sea, nicely laid out and furnished but a bit cramped, good restaurant. Sister hotel to the east coast **Atlantis Hotel**.

$$$$ Lone Star Motel, on the beach next to restaurant of same name, by **Royal Pavilion**, T419 0599, www.thelonestar.com. Refurbished under new ownership in 2013. 4 huge rooms with beachfront terraces, uncluttered, simple mahogany furniture, white linens and curtains, building was originally a garage built in 1940s by Romy Reid, who ran a bus company and called himself the Lone Star of the west coast, then it was a nightclub and then a house, owned by Mrs Robertson, of the jam company, who waterskied offshore until her late 80s.

$$$$ Sandy Lane, T444 2000, www.sandy lane.com. Most luxurious, expensive and pretentious hotel on the island. Golf, tennis, state-of-the-art spa with everything from detox to pedicures. It is worth going to the **L'Acajou** French restaurant or **Bajan Blue** or for Sun brunch buffet, 1230-1500, just to see the place (good food and not all that expensive), but you have to book ahead to get past the gate, T444 2030.

$$$$ Tamarind Cove, Paynes Bay, T432 1332, www.tamarindbarbados.com. 104 large rooms and suites overlooking pleasant gardens leading on to the beach, where there are comfy sun loungers and watersports. Good for couples or families. Indoor or outdoor dining, also **Daphne's** restaurant next door for a gourmet romantic dinner. Very comfortable hotel on 3 floors, spacious balconies, wheelchair access to ground floor rooms, internet access, water taxi to the sister properties in the **Elegant Hotels** group.

$$$$-$$$ Tropical Sunset (formerly Sunswept Beach Hotel), Holetown, T432 2715, www.sunsweptbeach.com. On the beach in town, great value for money considering the location, particularly out of season, 23 comfortable rooms, a/c, fan, TV, kitchenettes and balcony, small pool with direct access to sea, very convenient, lots of restaurants close by, shopping centre across the road, bank alongside, right in the centre of things for Holetown Carnival. Friendly staff, relaxed with no frills. Being refurbished 2013.

Apartments

$$$$-$$$ Calypso Rentals, Paynes Bay, T422 6405, www.calypso-rentals.com. Specializes in simple budget apartments and villas on the west coast. Some are right on the beach, others are a 5-min walk away from the water, whether they are pretty chattel houses or 6-bedroom villas with staff. If you are travelling in a group, it is possible to rent a property for as little as US$25 per person per day in summer.

$$$ Angler Apartments, Clarke's Rd, Derricks, T432 0817. Owners live on premises, priority given to service, friendly, informal, family orientated, rather tired furniture and linen, but clean and good budget option, 2-min walk to very private beach. Chandra is exceptionally helpful and will prepare your breakfast if you want. There are 5 friendly dogs.

$$$ Villa Marie Guesthouse, Lashley Rd, Fitts Village, St James, T417 5799, www.barbados.org/villas/villamarie. 3 large rooms, 2 apartments with kitchen (sleep 4), huge kitchen and dining room shared by all, well equipped, huge showers, pleasant garden with loungers and mature trees, barbecue, 5 mins' walk from supermarket and beach, very quiet, up side road, lots of repeat guests, run by Peter (German).

East Coast *p51, map p38*
$$$$ Atlantis, Tent Bay, Bathsheba, T433 9445, www.atlantishotelbarbados.com. Spectacular setting on the water's edge, waves crashing below, opened 1884 alongside railway, became a much-loved institution under the management of Enid Maxwell, who ran it from 1945-2001 and the place to go for Sun lunch. Now having had a facelift and refurbishment there are 8 rooms in the main building and two 2-bedroom suites by the pool. Friendly, welcoming service, comfortable. The tradition of Wed and Sun Bajan lunch buffets has been continued.

$$$$ Sea-U, Bathsheba, T433 9450, www.seaubarbados.com. The nicest place to stay on this side of the island, run by Uschi (German), colonial-style wooden house on top of cliffs, studio rooms with kitchenettes opening on to veranda with sea view, 2 studio apartments in separate cottage can be rented separately or as a single unit lots of hammocks between palm trees on the lawns or on balcony, quiet, peaceful, popular with active types who go to bed early. Ample buffet breakfast served in gazebo alongside main house, 3-course set menu dinner 5 nights a week, US$27.50.

$$$$-$$$ Round House Inn, Bathsheba, T433 9678, www.roundhousebarbados.com. Building dates from 1832 and overlooks the sea from the hillside, 4 rooms in round part, all different, one considerably nicer than the others with roof terrace, others cramped but light and bright, good restaurant, best place to eat in the evenings in the area, live music at weekends, run by Robert and Gail Manley.

South Coast *p56, map p38*
Most of the south coast is wall-to-wall hotels from Hastings to Dover popular with package holiday makers. It's close to the airport, with plenty of watersports and nightlife.

$$$$ Coral Sands, Worthing Beach, T435 6617, www.coralsandsresort.com. Attractive hotel, 30 large oceanfront studios (and penthouse 3-bed apartment), all with fully equipped kitchenettes, large balconies and good bathrooms, clean, comfortable. 5-min walk to **The Gap** for nightlife, 2-min walk to good supermarket. No entertainment at this quiet hotel, small pool overlooking the broad sandy beach. Take care with the current in the sea; no lifeguard.

$$$$ Crane Beach, T423 6220, www.the crane.com. Fairly near the airport, but definitely a taxi ride away, spectacular clifftop setting, glass elevator down to pink sand beach where there are sun loungers for guests, and good pool, 2 floodlit tennis courts, usually fairly quiet with only 18 luxury rooms in the old hotel, but an extra 250 timeshare units, have totally changed its character.

$$$$ Silver Point, Silver Sands, T420 4416, www.silverpointhotel.com. 10 mins' drive from the airport or The Gap. Rooms and suites with large balconies, microwave, fridge/freezer, on seafront with large area of decking over ironshore for daybeds and sun loungers, small pool, beach to the side. The sea is better for kitesurfing than swimming and this is a major area for the sport. Good but expensive restaurant, no alternatives in walking distance.

$$$$ Southern Palms, Christ Church, T428 7171, www.southernpalms.net. Short walk to all the restaurants and nightlife of The Gap. Comfortable and unpretentious beach hotel with rooms and spacious suites with kitchenettes. Popular with couples or families, mainly British guests, lovely stretch of beach.

$$$-$$ Beach House Cleverdale, 4th Av, Worthing, T428 3172, www.barbados-rentals.com. Looks like a chattel house from the outside, 15 m from Sandy Beach across vacant lot and short walk to beach bar. Versatile and affordable accommodation. Rent rooms or whole house, 5 double rooms, 4 have washbasins, 2 bathrooms, mosquito screens, large living/dining room with TV, stereo, use of kitchen, veranda and barbeque, also 1-bed self-catering studios attached, help with finding alternative self-catering accommodation if full, German-run.

Apartments

$$$$-$$$ Chateau Blanc Apartments On Sea, 1st Av, Worthing, T435 7518, www.chateaublancbarbados.com. Right on the beach, by **Carib Beach Bar**, close to restaurants and supermarkets, apartments range from seafront 1-2 bedrooms to seaview studios or rooms with kitchenettes. Good value, simple furnishings, a bit frayed around the edges but clean and well equipped, friendly management.

$$$ The Nook Apartments, Dayrells Rd in Rockley, T427 6502, www.thenookin barbados.com. Apartments and studios, small rooms, with large pool, maid service, secure, convenient for shops and restaurants, 2 mins from Accra/Rockley beach and the boardwalk.

$$$-$$ Maxwell Beach Apartments, Highway 7, Maxwell, T420 5387, or in the UK T01953-452136, www.apartmentsatmaxwell beach.com. Good location, on the beach. A 2-bedroom apartment or 3 1-bedroom studios, spacious, comfortable and well equipped, maid service every 5 days, good value for good quality. Walking distance to Oistins for Fish Fry, good for public transport, plenty of sun loungers in the garden overlooking the beach.

$$$-$$ Mike's Holiday Apartments/ Guesthouse, Landsdown, Silver Sands, T624 4725, www.barbadosmike.com. Studios or 1-bedroom small apartment, steps from the beach and windsurfing/ kitesurfing. Friendly family, helpful and informative. Simple accommodation but has everything you need for self-catering, good kitchens and bathrooms, Wi-Fi, ceiling fans, good value, cleaned weekly.

❷ Restaurants

Bridgetown *p24, map p26*
$$$ Brown Sugar, Bay St, Aquatic Gap, T426 7684. All-you-can-eat buffet lunch Sun to Fri 1200-1430, dinner daily from 1800. Bajan specialities, with items such as pumpkin fritters, breadfruit, pepperpot

and some good bread and butter pudding, filling and hearty, attractive setting, lots of greenery and waterfall.

$$$ Lobster Alive Bistro and Beach Bar, Carlisle Bay on beach, next to **Boatyard** on Bay St, T435 0305, www.lobsteralive.net. Daily 1200-2100. Mostly lobster flown in from the Grenadines and very expensive, but also other seafood such as crab backs, conch and chowder. Great for live jazz. Tables on the sand can get a bit windy. Parking is an issue with pushy men offering to watch your car for a tip.

$$$ Waterfront Café on the Careenage, T427 0093, www.diningwithus.net/waterfront. Lunch Mon-Sat 1000-1700, dinner Thu-Sat 1800-2100, drinks until 2400, closed Sun. Interesting food, plenty to look at with local art on the walls inside or boats outside in the sunshine and a good social centre in the evenings, live evening entertainment Thu-Sat Nov-Apr, less frequently in low season, mostly jazz.

$$ Balcony, upstairs in Cave Shepherd on Broad St. Lunch Mon-Fri 1100-1500. Go early because this is popular with locals and the queue gets long. Choose a small or large plate, pile it with salads, macaroni pie and all the trimmings, then pay for your portion of meat or fish and wash it down with a Banks beer. Great place to eat local food at local prices.

$$-$ Mustors Harbour, McGregor St, T426 5175. Mon-Fri 0900-1600. 3rd generation family business, snackette downstairs with Bajan fishcakes, flying fish cutters etc, restaurant upstairs, tasty, filling Bajan food. Specials include fried or stew chicken with rice and peas, mash potato or cou cou and salad for US$7.50.

Bridgetown: Garrison Historic Area *p29*

$$$ 39 Steps, the Chattel Plaza, Hastings Main Rd, at entrance to **Amaryllis Beach Resort** on the coast road near the Garrison, T427 0715, www.39stepsbarbados.com. Mon-Fri 1200-1500, Mon-Sat 1830-2300, last orders 2130, closed Sun and holidays. Wine

bar and restaurant, sit at the bar with a light bite or have a full meal at a table. Well run and lively, imaginative blackboard menu and choice of indoors or balcony, popular, so book at weekends. Live jazz 2 Sat evenings per month. Parking.

$ Cuz's Fish Shack, Needham's Point. Great fish cutters to fill a hole, fried marlin in a bread roll with some salad, cheese and egg optional extras or alternatives, wash it down with a beer for around US$5. Popular and there's usually a queue.

West Coast *p35*

$$$ Angry Annie's, 1st St, Holetown, T432 2119. Very colourful, informal, brightly painted, sociable host, dinner only, known for very good ribs, other dishes can be variable.

$$$ Café Indigo, Highway 1, Holetown, opposite Methodist Church, T432 0968. Open for breakfast and lunch 0800-1700. Upstairs in old building, full English US$10, pub lunch, US$8-12.50 main course, well-stocked bar.

$$$ The Cliff, Derricks, St James, T432 1922, www.thecliffbarbados.com. Dinner only, Mon-Sat, plus Sun in winter season. Worth the prices for a glimpse of the decor, stunning desserts, attractive and delightful meal, chef Paul Owens creates possibly the best food on the island but expect to pay at least US$125 for 2 courses per person with another US$20 for pudding.

$$$ Daphne's, Payne's Bay, T432 2731, www.daphnesbarbados.com. Open 1830-2200, cocktail bar open from 1700, happy hour 1700-1900. Italian, chic and contemporary, vegetarian and gluten-free menus available, try to get waterfront table when booking.

$$$ The Fish Pot, T439 3000, at Little Good Harbour Hotel, north of Speightstown, in 18th-century Fort Rupert. Imaginative menu, nice setting, comfortable, good service, reservations advised.

$$$ L'Attitude Beach Bar & Grill, Queen St, west end corner of Prince Alfred Lane, Speightstown, T422 0296/231 8502, see Facebook. Open 1000-1600. Nice waterfront setting by the mural, outdoor dining on the patio under canvas or umbrellas. Chef Gregory cooks everything on the barbecue, delicious local flavours, everything locally caught or grown, as organic as possible, great cocktails, spend a day on the beach, plenty of sun loungers and umbrellas. Check evening entertainment, often live music and dancing at weekends.

$$$ Lone Star, Mount Standfast, T419 0599, www.thelonestar.com. Open 1130-2230. Reopened end-2013 under new, British ownership, following a refurbishment. Italian and Caribbean fare, catch of the day, wood-fired pizza oven, cocktail bar and lounge, large deck, upmarket and chic beach restaurant.

$$$ The Mews, 2nd St, Holetown, T432 1122, www.themewsbarbados.com. Daily from 1800-2130, bar from 1730-late. Quite expensive but superb food, mix of local and French dishes, very pretty house, tables upstairs on balcony or interior patio. Bar with tapas menu downstairs. Live music, Wed, Fri, variety of styles.

$$$ Sitar, 2nd St, Holetown, T432 2248. Mon-Sat 1130-1430, daily 1800-2300. Indian, just the place for a tandoori or a hot vindaloo, although rather expensive.

$$$ The Tides, Holetown, T432 8356, www.tidesbarbados.com. Mon-Fri lunch, Mon-Sat dinner, reservations required. Seafood, meat and vegetarian dishes, served on an oceanfront terrace with a boardwalk between the tables and the sea, a/c lounge for drinks. Very highly thought of, one of the best restaurants on the island. Home to **On the Wall** art gallery.

$$$-$$ Mullins Beach Bar, Mullins Bay, just south of Speightstown, St Peter, T422 2044. Daily 1100-1900 for food, bar stays open later. The previous owners of **The Lone Star Motel**, Jason and Rory, have taken over this upmarket beach bar. All day menu for beach goers with service to your sun bed, also regular barbecues, music evenings and sporting events shown on big screen TV.

$$ Fisherman's Pub, Speightstown, T422 2703. Open 1000-1600, happy time 1600-1800, dinner 1800-2130 except Sun 1800-2200. A Speightstown institution which first opened to provide snacks and meals to local fishermen. Good Bajan meal and right on seafront, no frills, quick meal to go or stay and lime all afternoon, excellent fish cakes, Wed night dinner from 1900 with steel band and floor show from 2000 on the deck over sea.

$$ Patisserie Flindt, 1st St, Holetown, St James, T432 2626, www.flindtbarbados.com. Mon-Fri 0800-1700, Sat 0730-1600, Sun 0730-1200. Also smaller outlet in **Quayside Centre**, Rockley, T228 1759, Mon-Sat 0900-1700. 2 locations but the Holetown is the larger, with seating for breakfast, lunch or tea, or a snack at any time of day. The cakes, desserts and sweets in the patisserie are divine but pricey and the handmade chocolates are out of this world. Sandwiches, salads and pasta are on offer at lunchtime and they do a full English breakfast. Picnics can be made to order. Ideal for an event such as the Holders Season.

East Coast *p51*

There are a couple of beach bars on the east coast serving lunch, drinks and snacks: **Barclays Park Beach Bar** and **Sand Dunes**, Belleplaine, T422 9427. Open 0800-1600.

$$$ Naniki, Suriname, St Joseph, T433 1300, www.lushlife.bb. Lunch daily from 1230, jazz brunch buffet lunch on Sun, occasional moonlight dinners. Difficult to get to but well worth the effort, car or strong legs required, take turning off Highway 3 just south of St Joseph's church, signs to **Lush Life Nature Resort** (Naniki), on hillside overlooking Atlantic coast, great view over fields and palm trees, anthurium farm on property, cool and airy, eat on deck or inside, Sun buffet has good selection of Bajan dishes and great jazz from here or abroad, local ingredients, much of it organic, Bajan style, a special place, run by Tom Hinds.

$$$ Roundhouse Inn, Bathsheba (see Where to stay). Mon-Sat 0830-2030, Sun 0830-1700. Good, lovely location, overlooks sea, the best place to eat at night in the area, tasty starters, unusual combinations of ingredients, reggae Sat, live jazz Sun lunch.

South Coast *p56, map p38*
$$$ Champers, Skeetes Hill, Christ Church, T434 3463, www.champersbarbados.com. Mon-Sat 1130-late. Overlooking Accra beach, this is one of the best restaurants on the island. Waterfront dining upstairs on balcony, reservations essential to get the best tables, very good food and excellent service, summer 3-course menu for US$50. Plenty of car parking and facilities for wheelchair users.
$$$ Chopping Board Kitchen at MOJO, Worthing Main Rd, T435 9008, www.facebook.com/choppingboard. The place to come for a gourmet burger with hot, crispy fries. Steak, fish, pasta and other dishes are good too and prices are reasonable. Nice to sit out in the garden in the evening.
$$$ Pisces, St Lawrence Gap, T435 6439. Open 1800-2200. Perfect candlelit waterfront setting with waves lapping beneath you, good fish dishes, flying fish, lobster, also a prix fixe menu for US$45, very popular, staff rushed off their feet, service suffers.
$$$-$$ Café Sol, St Lawrence Gap, T420 7655, www.cafesolbarbados.com. Lunch Tue-Sun from 1130, dinner every night. Happy hours 1700-1900, 2200-2400, 2 for 1 drinks specials all night. Mexican American, grill and **Margarita** bar, 15 flavours of margaritas, by the glass US$7 or by the jug US$28, Very popular, all the usual TexMex dishes, nachos, fajitas, tacos, also appetizers/tapas for good value snacks. Partnered with **McBride's Irish Pub**.
$$$-$$ Carib Beach Bar, Worthing, T435 8540. Open from 1100, happy hour Mon-Fri 1700-1800, last orders from kitchen 2145. Quite an institution now, this laid-back beach bar on a lovely stretch of sand is popular with locals and visitors, nothing fancy, plastic chairs, unpretentious.

Inexpensive meals and drinks, local dishes such as flying fish, fish cakes, or burgers, sandwiches, pasta and suchlike. barbecue and music twice a week, excellent rum punches, great fun even if you are not eating. Sunbeds and umbrellas for hire on the beach.

◑ Bars and clubs

The website www.barbados.org/whatson inbarbados has a list of what's on every day and night of the week. Most clubs charge more for entry on 'free drinks' night, less when you are paying for the drinks. It's worth phoning in advance to find out what is on offer. There are live bands on certain nights in some clubs. Most do not get lively until almost midnight, and close around 0400. Some have a complicated set of dress codes or admission rules, which is another reason for phoning ahead.
The Boatyard, T436 2622, www.theboatyard.com, is on the beach at Carlisle Bay, Bay St, an all-day, all-night party venue for cruise ship passengers and then stayover visitors, with water toys, sun beds, games, music and dancing. Bar and restaurant on the sand, daily and nightly specials, check Facebook to see what's on.
Bubba's Sports Bar & Restaurant, Rockley Main Rd, T435 6217, www.bubbassportsbar.net. Mon-Thu 1130-2300, Fri-Sat 1100-0100, Sun 0800-2300, Has 3 10-ft screens plus 12 other TVs for watching sports while you drink.
Harbour Lights, Marine Villa, Bay St, T436 7225, www.harbourlightsbarbados.com. Good for families early on, then a younger crowd later, lots of tourists and expats, open-air on the beach, local and disco music, crowded. Wed and Fri night club, entry covers 'free' drinks Wed 2100-0200, Fri 2130-0300, Mon and Wed beach party with dinner and show with fire eaters, stilt walkers, acrobats, tuk band, limbo dancers, with a finale of steel pan and dancers, all ages 1900-2230, drinking continues after

then, drinks included until 2400, ticket price includes hotel transfers there and back.
Lexy Piano Bar, at the end of 2nd St, Holetown, T432 5399, www.lexypiano bar.com. Open from 1830, nightly in season, live entertainment 2100-0200, singing, dancing, a good time is had by all. Owned by Alex Santoriello, former Broadway performer and producer, the club attracts locals, tourists and celebrities including Prince Harry, who took a shine to the bar.
McBride's Irish Pub, St Lawrence Gap, T420 7646, see Facebook for what's on. Has DJ or live music every night. Partnered with **Café Sol**, synchronized happy hours.
Old Jamm Inn, St Lawrence Gap, T428 3919, see Facebook. Open 'til 0300-0400. Offering 'booze, beats and burgers' this lounge bar with outdoor deck delivers good food to go with the music and drinks. Live and DJ music, sometimes jazz, sometimes reggae, varied line-up. Located on site of previous clubs, **After Dark** and **Lipgloss**.
PRIVA, 1st St, Holetown, T836 2165, www.privabarbados.com. Thu-Sat 2200-0400, Sun 1800-0100. Lounge club with bottle service, late night dancing, DJs, book a front line table close to the main bar and DJs if you're in a group of up to 10, or for something quieter the terrace garden has beds where you can lounge and chat. There's also a VIP suite for parties of up to 30. Chic club, made headlines when Rihanna booked it for a private party in 2013.
Reggae Lounge, St Lawrence Gap, T435 6462. Sun-Wed 2000-0300, Thu-Sat 2000-0400. A bit sleezy but can be fun, different happenings every night, DJ for mix of music or live reggae band, music videos on big screen, events change with the season, bartender pours strong drinks, restaurant alongside.
Sugar Ultra Lounge, St Lawrence Gap, T420 7662, see Facebook. Tue, Sat 2200-0300, Thu 2200-0400. Ibiza-style club with light show wall, VIP areas and white leather sofas. DJ, good mix of house, techno, trance, dub, then live bands on the last Tue of month.

Rumshops

If you drink in a rumshop, rum and other drinks are bought by the bottle. The smallest size is a mini, then a flask, then a full bottle. The shop will supply ice and glasses, you buy a mixer, and serve yourself. Wine, in a rumshop, usually means sweet sherry. If you are not careful, it is drunk with ice and beer. **Baxters Rd** in Bridgetown never sleeps. The one-roomed, ramshackle, rumshops are open all night, and there's a lot of street life after midnight. Some of the rumshops sell fried chicken (the **Pink Star** is recommended, it has a large indoor area and clean lavatories) and there are women in the street selling fish, seasoned and fried in coconut oil over an open wood fire. Like Oistins, but every night. Especially recommended if you are hungry after midnight but keep your wits about you, this is not a tourist area.

Oistins on a Fri night is a major event for both Bajans and tourists. Lots of shops selling fish meals and other food, dub music one end and at the other a small club where they play oldies for ballroom dancing. It continues on Sat and Sun, though a bit quieter, some food places also stay open through the week. In the north of the island there is a smaller fish fry at Half Moon Fort, just north of Little Good Harbour, with tuna, barracuda, kingfish, next to the beach and under a breadfruit tree. Fri, Sat and Sun 1800 till very late. Also good is **Fisherman's Pub** on the waterfront in **Speightstown**, lots of music on Wed (see above).

Party cruises

The Jolly Roger 1, Black Pearl Party Cruises, Carlisle House, Bridgetown, T436 2885, www. barbadosblackpearl-jollyroger1.com. Run 4-hr daytime and evening cruises along the west coast to Holetown, near the Folkestone Underwater Park (where the fun and games take place) from the deepwater harbour. The drinks are unlimited. There is also a meal, music, dancing, etc. On daytime cruises, there is swimming and snorkelling.

The Monkey Jar

A monkey jar is a traditional vessel for storing drinking water and keeping it cool in the days before fridges. Known as a 'monkey' it is made from local terra cotta clay and fired to 1100°C. The clay is slightly porous, allowing some of the water to penetrate it and make the exterior very cold, which in turn keeps the water inside cool. It looks more like a teapot than a monkey or a jar, but some potters decorate and customize the jar with monkey attributes for the tourist market.

Entertainment

Cinemas
Globe drive-in, off ABC Highway, T437 0480. **Limegrove Cinemas**, Holetown, T420 2000, www.limegrovecinemas.com. **Olympus Theatres Multiplex**, Sheraton Mall, Christ Church, T437 1000, www.olympus.bb.

Shopping

Prices are high, but the range of goods available is excellent. Travellers who are going on to other islands may find it useful to do some shopping here. If coming from another Caribbean island there are strict controls on bringing in fresh fruit and vegetables.

Duty-free shopping is well advertised. Visitors who produce a passport and air ticket can take most duty-free goods away from the store for use in the island before they leave, but not camera film or alcohol. Cameras and electrical goods may be cheaper in an ordinary discount store in the USA or Europe than duty free in Barbados. A duty-free shopping centre for cruise ship passengers is inside the deep water harbour, the **Bridgetown Cruise Terminal**.

Art galleries
Barbados Arts Council, Pelican Craft Village, Bridgetown, T426 4385, www.barbados artscouncil.com. Daily 0900-2130. A non-profit organization set up to foster Barbadian art and artists. Works exhibited at these galleries are drawn from its 300 members, both established artists with an international reputation and those just starting out. **Gallery of Caribbean Art**, Northern Business Centre, Queen St, Speightstown, T419 0858, www.artgallerycaribbean.com. Mon-Fri 0930-1630, Sat 0930-1400. A range of contemporary regional art work.

Crafts
Best of Barbados, Chattel Village in Holetown, Southern Palms Hotel in St Lawrence Gap, Quayside Centre in Rockley, the airport departure lounge and the Bridgetown Cruise Terminal, www.best-of-barbados.com. The ultimate gift shop with every Barbados souvenir imaginable. The designs mostly stem from the work of Jill Walker, who has been living and painting in Barbados since 1955, and they have a network of cottage workers making things exclusively for the shop. Her prints of local scenes are on sale, mugs, candles and T-shirts. **Earthworks Pottery**, Edgehill Heights No 2, St Thomas, T425 0223, www.earthworks-pottery.com. Mon-Fri 0900-1700, Sat 0900-1300. The best place to come for local pottery you can actually use: solid houseware and pots in blues and greens with several different designs, mix and match square, round and rectangular dishwasher-safe crockery, used in local cafés. VAT-free for visitors. Everything is hand made and you can see the potters at work. They will make commissioned pieces. Also on the property are **On The Wall Art Gallery**, **Arthouse Café**, **Batik Studio** and **Ins and Outs Gift Emporium**. **Pelican Craft Centre**, Princess Alice Highway near the harbour. Mon-Fri

0900-1800, Sat 0900-1400. Good displays of craft items, all made in Barbados, at over 25 shops in replica chattel houses where you can watch artisans at work. **Red Clay Pottery** and **Fairfield Gallery**, Fairfield Cross Rd, just outside Bridgetown, T424 3800, see Facebook. Sell very good ceramics. Family business using local clay to make ceramic art, crockery and garden pots in an old syrup boiling house. Demonstration and tour.

Groceries

Supercentre is the biggest of the chain supermarkets with 5 stores: at Sunset Crest in Holetown, in the Warrens Shopping Complex off the ABC Highway, the south coast branches of **Big B** in the Peronne Village, Rendezvous, Christ Church and **Supercentre Oistins**, Southern Plaza, Oistins, and finally **JB's Supercentre** situated in Sargent's Village, Christ Church. **Jordan's Supermarket** have 4 branches, of which the largest are in Fitt's Village and Speightstown. There are many other supermarkets, convenience stores and farmers' markets. Nearly all food is imported, so expensive.

⚙ What to do

The people of Barbados are sport mad and the facilities for pursuing a sport of your choice are excellent for an island of this size. Cricket still draws the largest following and there are dozens of famous cricketers considered household names. Going to watch a cricket match is an entertaining cultural experience and well worth doing, even if you don't understand the game. Football and rugby are also played and followed enthusiastically by the crowd. An unusual spectator sport for a Caribbean island is horse racing, which is exciting to watch, but even more extraordinary is polo, which appears to have been dropped in from the Home Counties and is followed avidly by mostly white ex-pats. Participation sports are also well developed and there are great facilities for visitors to play golf, tennis and several other sports. The sea is a natural water playground and you can scuba dive, sail, fish, windsurf, kitesurf and surf as well as hire more low key water toys on the beach. Sports tourism is very popular, with youth and adult teams from the UK and other countries travelling to play matches in Barbados. Contact the **National Sports Council**, Blenheim, St Michael, T436 6127, www.nsc barbados.com, for more information.

Athletics

Sir Garfield Sobers Sports Complex, Wildey, St Michael, T437 6016, www. gymnasiumltd.com.bb. A multi-purpose gymnasium offering badminton, bodybuilding, boxing, basketball, gymnastics, handball, judo, karate, netball, table tennis, volleyball and weightlifting. There are plenty of changing rooms and showers, also sauna and massage rooms, a medical room and warm-up/practice area. Adjacent is the **Aquatic Centre**, T429 7946, with a 10-lane Olympic-size swimming pool, tennis courts, hockey, football and cricket pitches outside.

Board games

Chess, draughts (US=Checkers), dominoes and warri are played to a high standard. Join a rum shop match at your peril. The best domino 'slammers' compete in a league and the national team has won the world championship several times. Barbados has a world champion draughts player, Ronald 'Suki' King. The island's Sports Person of the Year 2001 was the first Barbadian chess player to reach the rank of International Master, 34-year-old Kevin Denny. Warri is a board game which has been around since time immemorial and has been traced to the ancient Kush civilizations on the Upper Nile. It is believed to have come over to the Caribbean with the slaves. Lee Farnum-Badley, T432 1292, makes and sells warri boards and provides expert tuition. **The Barbados Bridge League**, T427 4839, www.bridgewebs.com/barbadosleague, offers bridge most nights and organizes competitions throughout the year, the biggest of which is the Sun, Sea and Slams Tournament in Feb, which attracts players from all over the world.

Cricket

Cricket is King in Barbados and everybody has an opinion on the state of the game as well as the latest results. There is lots of village cricket all over the island at weekends. A match here is nothing if not a social occasion. Great Bajan cricketers become icons and 5 have been knighted for their services to the game and their country: Sir Garfield Sobers (the only living National Hero), Sir Conrad Hunte, Sir Everton Weekes, Sir Clyde Walcott and Sir Frank Worrell. In addition to Test Matches and inter-island competitions there are tournaments for the young and old: the Sir Garfield Sobers International Schools Tournament and the Sir Garfield Sobers Seniors Cricket Festival being 2 of the most important. Barbados is the premier cricket tour destination in the world and cricket lovers should try to arrange their visit to coincide with a Test Match or a One Day International at the new Kensington Oval. For the **Cricket World Cup** in 2007, Barbados hosted the Final at the Oval. This historic ground first hosted a Test Match in 1929-1930, but for the CWC had a major upgrade to add extra seats and improve facilities for the players, media and sponsors. No sedate Sunday afternoon crowd this – the atmosphere is electric – with DJ music, constant whistling, horn-blowing, cheering and banter. Everything stops for a Test Match and offices are empty of workers, who are in 'meetings' all day. At lunch there are food stalls outside where you can pick up a burger, roti or Bajan stew, buy a T-shirt and West Indies hat and drink a few Banks beers. The biggest crowds come for the matches against England, with touring teams tagging along, but cricket tourists come from as far as Australia or South Africa.

For information about the bigger matches at Kensington Oval phone the **Barbados Cricket Association**, T426 2018, www.bcacricket.org, or the West Indies Cricket Board, T4251093, www.windiescricket.com. If you and your local team want to tour Barbados, contact **Sporting Barbados**, T228 9122, www.sportingbarbados.com, for help with discounts and keeping the costs down or to put you in touch with a specialist tour agency.

Diving

Although Barbados is among the more developed islands in the Caribbean, reef life is not as bad as might be expected and some reefs are thriving. Within the last few years the island has become known as a wreck diving destination. Several shipwrecks have been intentionally sunk as diving sites, offering interesting underwater photography, in addition to the many ships which have sunk in storms or battles during the life of this seafaring nation. Barbados is surrounded by an inner reef and an outer barrier reef. On the west coast the inner reef is within swimming distance for snorkelling or learning to dive, while the outer reef is a short boat ride away and the water is deeper. Here you can see barracuda, king fish, moray eels, turtles and squid as well as some fine black coral, barrel sponges and sea fans. The underwater landscape may not be as pristine as some other islands, but there are some excellent wrecks worth exploring and Carlisle Bay is littered with bottles, cannon balls, anchors and small items such as buckles and buttons after many centuries of visiting ships 'losing' things overboard or sinking. There are 200 reported wrecks in Carlisle Bay, but another popular dive site is the *Stavronikita* in the Folkestone Marine Park, one of the best diving wrecks in the Caribbean. Scuba diving to reefs or wrecks around the coast can be arranged with a number of companies on the south and west coasts. They offer PADI courses, equipment rental and other facilities. The **Barbados Sub Aqua Club**,

Cricket in the Caribbean

Cricket in the Caribbean is a game played to a backdrop of rapturous music, stomach-tingling food, fervent politics and joyous partying. It is played in front of the most knowledgeable spectators in the world, who will stop you in the street to provide a breakdown of tactics and techniques (or their absence) in West Indian batting. It is played in the sun (mostly). It is played to laughter.

The six first-class teams are: Jamaica, Trinidad and Tobago, Barbados, Guyana, Windward Islands and Leeward Islands. Inter-island matches are hugely entertaining, with a one-day competition before Christmas and the four-day Regional Four Day Competition from January to March. Unless the West Indies side is on tour, all the international players are required to play in the competition, so the standard is high. Consult www. caribbeancricket.com, www.windies cricket.com, or www.cricinfo.com.

The West Indies hosted the six-week **Cricket World Cup** in 2007, with matches played in Antigua and Barbuda, Barbados, Grenada, Guyana, Jamaica, St Kitts and Nevis, St Lucia and Trinidad and Tobago, while warm-up matches were also played in St Vincent. All these islands now have superb facilities with totally new or completely refurbished grounds and there is a wealth of choice of venues for Test Matches, One-Day Internationals or other world-class cricket.

The development of cricket and of the West Indies team in the English-speaking Caribbean during the 20th century reflected the political struggle for Independence. The best cricketers became respected role models. Learie Constantine, a barrister and advocate of cricketers' rights, paved the way in the 1920s and 1930s. Lightning fast bowler, cavalier batsman, the finest fielder in the world, he was loved and revered from Trinidad to England. He captained the Dominions cricket team that played against England in the series immediately following World War II; a massive recognition at that stage of the 20th century for a black man in a white-dominated team.

The great Jamaican batsman, George Headley, became the first black person to captain the West Indies side in 1948. He paved the way for Frank Worrell, another believer in players' rights, who was the first fully appointed black captain of the West Indies a decade later. The first West Indies win in England brought joyous acclaim in 1950 and new respect in the English-speaking world. Worrell, with his two seminal series as captain in Australia in 1960-1961 and England in 1963, brought a unity to the Caribbean and a consistency to the team that lasted for over 35 years. Sir Garry Sobers remains arguably the greatest cricketer yet born. The dominance of Clive Lloyd and Viv Richards in the 1970s and '80s, both in batting and captaincy, took the West Indies to a new level. The bowling of Roberts, Garner, Holding, Marshall, Ambrose and Walsh struck both fear and admiration into many an armchair spectator, let alone the batsmen who faced them. For over a decade, West Indies cricket has been in decline. Only the batting brilliance of Brian Lara kept the side from complete annihilation but he retired in 2007 after the World Cup. The team's most recent success was to win the ICC World Twenty20 Championship in 2012.

a branch of the British Sub Aqua Club (BSAC), www.bsac.com, meets at 0800 on Sun at the **Boatyard Pub**, on the waterfront on Bay St, Bridgetown. They don't hire out equipment but if you have your own they are welcoming to members from other branches, T421 6020, Rob Bates. There is a recompression chamber at St Anne's Fort, T427 8819, inform the operator of an emergency.

Atlantis Submarines Barbados is at Shallow Draft Harbour, T436 8929, www.barbados.atlantissubmarines.com. For those who want to see the underwater world without getting wet. The day and night dives cost US$104 and US$114 respectively, discounts in low season. The tour starts with a short video and then you go by bus to the deep water port or join the launch at the Careenage. The boat takes about 10 mins to get to the submarine, sit at the front to be first on the sub, an advantage as then you can see out of the driver's window as well as out of your own porthole. 2 divers on underwater scooters join the submarine for the last 15 mins, putting on a dive show. The 1730 'night' dive is the best as the submarine turns on its lights which bring out pretty colours not seen by daylight. Booking is necessary, check in 30 mins before dive time; whole tour takes 1½ hrs.

Barbados Blue, T434 5734, www.dive barbadosblue.com. Providing water sports at the Hilton Hotel with non-motorized sports free to guests. Like many dive operators they are involved in trying to eradicate the invasive lion fish by fishing and eating it. Dive trips at 1000, 1200, 1400, 1 tank US$70, 2 tanks US$120, Open Water certification course US$430, 10% discount on diving with your own gear.

Eco-Dive Barbados, T243 5816, www.ecodivebarbados.com. Specialize in small groups, personalized service including hotel transfers, all equipment, snacks and drinks. They charge US$75 for a single tank dive, US$125 for 2 tanks and US$430 for an Open Water certification course.

West Side Scuba Centre, Mowbray, Hastings Main Rd, T262 1029, www.west sidescuba.com. Friendly team, good service, very safety conscious and dive by the book. Single tank dives US$60, 2 tanks US$110, all gear included, Open Water course US$432. Diving mostly the south and west coasts, in the summer they dive the east coast where you can see larger fish and different underwater terrain.

Fishing

Charter boats for game fishing are lined up along the Careenage, Bridgetown, so you can inspect the goods before deciding who to call.

Barbados Game Fishing Association, www.barbadosgamefishing.com. Runs the Barbados International Fishing Tournament in Apr at Port St Charles. The targets are blue marlin, yellow fin tuna, white marlin, sailfish, wahoo and dolphin fish (mahi mahi).

Golf

Many keen golfers come here just to play golf and there are enough courses to keep anyone busy for a while with 5 18-hole and 2 9-hole courses. The RBTT Golf Classic is held in Nov; the Barbados Pro-Am Golf Tournament in Dec; the Sir Garfield Sobers Festival of Golf Championships in Apr (played on 3 courses with 240 players including former Test cricketers, celebrities and professional golfers) and other competitions throughout the year.

Apes Hill Club, Apes Hill, St James, T432 4500, www.apeshillclub.com. A par-72 championship course high up in the hills with a tremendous view, but not only is it a beautiful and challenging course, one of the best in the world, but it is a certified Audubon Cooperative Sanctuary for its environmental and wildlife conservation work.

Barbados Golf Club, T428 1281, www.barbadosgolfclub.com. Open to the public, 18-hole course, at Durants, Christ Church. Green fee US$105 Jan-Jun, less in low season, also tuition, 3- and 7-day passes, etc.

Royal Westmoreland Golf and Country Club, St James, T419 7242, www.royalwest moreland.com. An 18-hole, par 72 course spread over 480 acres on a hilly site in St James with views over the west coast. To play here you must be staying in one of the villas or at a hotel with an access agreement or be the guest of a member. For non-residents/guests, limited access is available Sun-Fri 1000-1100. Members can use the hotel's beach club facilities 5 mins' drive away. 3 club houses, a swimming pool and 5 tennis courts.

Sandy Lane, T444 2514, www.sandy lane.com. Traditionally the best and most prestigious of the championship courses, has 2, 18-hole courses and a 9-hole course, all on 600 acres of former sugar cane land next to the hotel. Tiger Woods got married on the course here.

Hiking

The most beautiful part of the island is the Scotland District on the east coast. There is also some fine country along the St Lucy coast in the north and on the southeast coast. There is a particularly good route along the old railway track from Bath to Bathsheba and on to Cattlewash. **The National Trust**, www.barbados nationaltrust.org. Organizes free Sun walks at 0600, 1530 and 1730 (depending on moon). 3 speeds: 'stop and stare', 8-10 km, 'here and there', 13-15 km, 'grin and bear', 19-21 km. Their walk to Chalky Mount in the Scotland District has been recommended. Stephen Mendes, of **Hike Barbados**, T230 4818, www.hikebarbados.com, offers guided scenic walks of 3-16 km for US$150-250, regardless of numbers of hikers.

Hockey

Hockey is played on an astroturf hockey pitch at the Sir Garfield Sobers Sports Complex, Wildey, St Michael, but there are also matches at the Kensington Oval cricket ground, BET Sports Club and Banks Breweries. **Banks International Hockey Festival** is the largest event of its type in the Americas and is held over a week in Aug with 37 local teams and some 26 from overseas. Other hockey events are arranged around this time for touring sides, whether schools or clubs. Contact the Barbados Hockey Federation, www.barbadoshockey.org.

Horseracing

The Barbados Turf Club, T626 3980, www.barbadosturfclub.com. Holds flat race meetings at the Garrison on Sat during 3 seasons (Jan-Mar, May-Oct and Nov-Dec). The biggest one being the Sandy Lane Gold cup held in Mar, which features horses from neighbouring islands. Again, this is something of a social occasion, with parties, parades and concerts. The Royal Barbados Mounted Police band leads a parade of dancers, tumblers and stiltmen in carnival fashion. Horse racing dates back to colonial days when planters challenged each other to races. Later the cavalry officers of the British army joined in and by 1840 there were regular race days at the Garrison. If you can't get to a race meet you can watch training sessions at the Garrison just after 0600 when the weather is still cool. Races are held in the heat of the day from 1330. Admission to the grandstand is US$7.50 but you can get a good view from various points around the track where there are betting shops and food and drink stalls. The track is just under a mile long, oval shaped with a 2-furlong finishing straight. Horses run clockwise.

Paddle boarding

Paddle Barbados, T249 2787, www.paddle barbados.com. Stand-up paddle boarding (SUP) has take off in Barbados in a big way. SUP lessons are held in Carlisle Bay, but you can rent a board or book a tour to paddle where you please. Tours of 2-4 hrs are arranged on the west, south or east coasts, according to levels of skill and experience. There are lots of good locations for the sport. A variety of boards can be supplied according to your needs.

Horsing around

The first Saturday in March is a special day in Barbados' calendar. It has nothing to do with Carnival, being celebrated in neighbouring Trinidad and other islands, but you might be forgiven for thinking it has. Head for the Garrison and you'll see dancers, stilt walkers, gymnasts, singers, celebrities and regimental bands. There are crowds, stalls, noise, merriment and lots of entertainment.

This is the Sandy Lane Gold Cup.

Horse racing is surprisingly popular on the Caribbean islands where there is sufficient flat land to build a race track and even on some where there isn't. Like many sports it is seen as an opportunity for a party and the crowd is enthusiastic, even if not particularly knowledgeable, although never underestimate the locals when it comes to betting.

There are nine races on Gold Cup day and it is the biggest day in the Barbados Turf Club's programme, attracting famous names from home and abroad. There is as much to look at off the track as on it. Dating back to 1982, it is now firmly established on the racing calendar, with the event attracting some of the top British jockeys and those from Barbados now racing in Canada, such as Patrick Husbands, who has been Champion Jockey seven times in that country. There is huge (and friendly) rivalry between the owners, breeders and trainers, which of course filters down to the grooms and stable hands and their friends and families in the crowd and backstage.

The Main Stand gives you a good vantage point, but anywhere around the track is good to watch the racing. You can get right up close to the action by the parade ring, the finish line or the jockeys making their way to the weighing room, the betting booths are never far away and there is entertainment from 1300-1800. The most important race is the penultimate one and all the excitement builds up to see who will win the gold trophy, traditionally flown in from London by British Airways and on display beside the parade ring until it is moved to the President's Box of the Barbados Turf Club and then presented to the winner by the Prime Minister of Barbados.

Polo

Polo has been played since cavalry officers introduced the game in the 19th century and the Polo Club was formed in 1884. The sport used to be played at the Garrison, where ponies were often reject race horses, but in 1965 it moved to Holders Hill and its popularity has steadily risen since then. The polo season runs from Jan-May and the island has a reputation for its hospitality and social events. International matches are held at Apes Hill (formerly Waterhall), Holders and Lion Castle, although there are two other fields: Buttals Polo Field and Clifton Polo Ground. Matches are weather-dependent, so call ahead if in doubt.

Apes Hill Polo Club, Apes Hill, St James, T262 3282 (Jamie Dickson), www.apeshill polobarbados.com. Entry on match days US$10 adults, US$5 children, tea and refreshments and a full bar available. Riders can also have a 1-hr polo lesson for US$235 with a qualified polo instructor and take part in a chukka.

Barbados Polo Club, Holders Hill, St James, T432 1802, www.barbadospoloclub.com. US$10 entrance with food and drinks available, good commentary and a great way to spend a couple of hours even if you know nothing about polo.

Lion Castle Polo Club, Lion Castle, St Thomas, T622 7656, see Facebook. Polo is played here between Nov-May, adults

Polo

The Empire's finest colonial traditions were alive and kicking. The ladies wore their crisp cotton dressed and high heels, the gentlemen were in neatly pressed shirts and bermuda shorts. Tea in bone china cups and cucumber sandwiches were available in the clubhouse. The band struck up and everybody stood smartly to attention as they played the British national anthem in honour of the visiting team, followed by the Barbados national anthem for the home side. A moment's silence was observed in memory of a recently departed long-serving member of the club, followed by a prayer for good sport. The horses fidgeted impatiently, but finally they were allowed to start the game, which was fast and furious. The commentator's patter was informative, interspersed with comments about the backside of one of the competitors, Lucy, the only woman on a horse, playing for Cheshire, the British side. The polo ponies charged up and down, wheeling around on a sixpence and setting off in the opposite direction at a touch from their riders.

The home side, the Brigands, took an early lead, but Cheshire hung on to push for a nail-biting end to the match. Prize giving was elaborate as expected with the award of the Mercedes Benz Challenge Shield. The sponsors were much in evidence, with several models of their cars on display, and many more in the car park, but real horse power probably outnumbered the Mercedes. There are 154 polo ponies on the island and at least half of them were at Holders that evening, with an almost equivalent number of young, black, stable hands to care for them, hosing them down after their exertions and preparing the next ones to do battle. A jolly time was had by ex-pats and white Bajans during and after the match. The bar did brisk business and after the ladies of the club had served tea, they turned their hands to a barbeque in honour of the visiting team and their families on holiday in Barbados. A major social event in Little England, polo remains the sport of the affluent elite, wherever it is played, and a spectacle for visitors and outsiders.

US$10, children US$5, children under 12 free, full bar, tea and refreshments, very grand clubhouse.

Riding
There are riding schools offering beach and/or country rides. Some do not give instruction and cater for pleasure riding only. **Barbados Equestrian Association**, www.barbadosequestrian.com. Dressage events organized by the Association are all held at Congo Road, near Six Roads. The BEA is FEI-affiliated.

Road tennis
This is a local game with defined rules, played with a low wooden 'net' on some minor (and some main) roads and a court marked out with chalk, although there are now more professional courts and professional players. It is rather like a cross between tennis and table tennis, played with wooden bats and a skinned tennis ball. The World Road Tennis Series is held at the end of Nov. For information contact the **Professional Barbados Road Tennis Association**, T245 3953, www.proroadtennis.com.

Running
Running became more popular in Barbados when sprinter Obadele Thompson won an Olympic bronze medal and hurdler Andrea Blackett won gold at the Commonwealth Games. All levels of fitness enthusiasts

The rise of rugby

The Garrison Savannah was once a swamp before it was drained by the Royal Engineers to become a parade ground for soldiers and the place where they trained and drilled. Two hundred years later, it is still used for physical training, but of a recreational nature, and it still sometimes resembles a swamp. Some days you can find horses racing around the track while at the same time a rugby match, a football tournament or a game of cricket is being held.

Rugby arrived in the 1960s when teams of ex-pats and locals were assembled to play against visiting naval teams. While the navy was in port there were hard and enthusiastic games followed by equally hard and enthusiastic, alcohol-fuelled celebrations. Even today there are match fixtures against visiting ships. The first rugby pitch was also used for polo, so that inevitably frequently became a mud bath until an ex-pat, rugby-playing architect designed a soak-away. The first club house was the back of someone's Land Rover, lacking in running water but well stocked with alternative refreshment. Funds were eventually raised for a proper club house, partly through staging an annual pantomime at St Winifred's School. As in the UK, there was an affinity with cricket players and many of them swelled the ranks of rugby enthusiasts.

With an energetic committee organizing the sport, the development of rugby on Barbados progressed steadily. The sport was introduced in schools and fed through into the adult teams, both male and female. There are now four main clubs on the island and they play throughout the year, at home and abroad in regional competitions, while providing players for West Indian 15- and seven-a-side teams. Visiting school and club teams find a warm welcome, both on and off the field. There may still be mud but there will also be hot showers, and there will definitely still be some hard partying afterwards.

Barbados Rugby Football Union, www.rugbybarbados.com.

practice early morning at the Garrison. The **Run Barbados Series**, www.run barbados.org, is held in early Dec and is comprised of: a fun mile, 3 km, 5 km, 10 km and a half marathon. This has proved so popular that entries have risen from 300 in 1999 to over 1000 now. Less ambitiously also Hash Harriers, Sat, with a run or walk of 1-2 hrs, followed by barbecue and drinks, T826 5575, www.barbadoshash.com

Sailing
Barbados Yacht Club, Carlisle Bay, T427 1125, www.barbadosyachtclub.com. Holds regattas and offers sailing courses. Sailing can be a bit choppy along the south coast to Oistins and most races head up the west coast where the waters are calmer. The 3-day Annual Mount Gay Rum Boatyard Regatta in May is the main event of the year. Carlisle Bay is the main anchorage and focal point for the sailing fraternity.

There are lots of motor and sailing boats available for charter by the week, day or for shorter periods. A cruise up the west side of the island with stops for snorkelling and swimming with turtles are very popular, whether for lunch or sunset watching. While they all follow more or less the same route, and unfortunately they all feed the turtles and fish to get them to come close, the experience can differ widely. The larger catamarans can be cheaper than the smaller ones but they are often packed to the gunnels and can feel crowded. On a less busy day they are enjoyable, but it is difficult to find out how booked each cruise is likely to be. When cruise ships are in port, the catamarans are very busy with 50-100 guests on board. Those boats that limit numbers are likely to be more friendly and relaxed with better service.

The Elegance Cruises, T830 4218, www.elegancebarbados.com. Lunch cruise 0930-1430, US$100, sunset dinner cruise 1700-1900, US$90, number of guests limited to 14, also private charters. Includes taxi transfers, all food and drinks, snorkelling equipment, gentle music. Snorkel over wrecks and swim with turtles, attentive crew accompany you in the water, good food, free-flowing drinks, both alcoholic and non-alcoholic.

The Sail Calabaza, T826 4048, www.barbadossailingcruises.com. Luxury catamaran taking a maximum of 12 guests for a comfortable and friendly tour of the west coast leaving from the Careenage, Bridgetown, stopping to snorkel over a couple of wrecks before swimming with the turtles. A crew member always accompanies swimmers in the water, takes photos and emails them to you along with some Bajan recipes. Excellent food, snacks, drinks, served on china and in glasses, not plastic. Very conservation-minded crew, full of stories and information, offering sunset cruises 1500-1830, US$90 adults, US$75 children under 12, lunch cruises 0930-1430, US$110 adults, US$90 children, or private cruises.

The Silver Moon Catamaran, T435 5285, www.silvermoonbarbados.com. Luxury catamarans with a maximum capacity of 12 (US$115) or 24 (US$92.50) guests, so a group can easily block book. Very popular with cruise passengers so day cruises are often heavily booked. Sails 0930-1430 or 1500-2000 up the west coast with snorkelling stops. Good food and drinks. Private charters can be arranged.

Squash

Barbados Squash Association, Olympic Centre, Garfield Sobers Sports Complex, www.squashbarbados.org. There are players of all levels on Barbados who will happily give you or your team a game.

Surfing

The best surfing is on the east coast at the Soup Bowl, Bathsheba, which has the most consistent break. The best time is Aug-Nov when you get perfect barrelling waves. Experienced surfers also like Duppies on the north coast, where you have a long paddle out and there is a lot of current, but the waves are really big. The south coast is good for beginners and for boogie boarding, although there is a good break at Brandons, while the west coast has some good spots with good access, often best when there are no waves on the east coast. Sandy Lane, Tropicana, Gibbs and Maycocks are all worth trying. The Barbados International Surfing Championship is held at the Soup Bowl, Bathsheba, in late Nov, contact the Barbados Surfing Association, www.barbadossurfingassociation.org.

Boosy's Surf School, T267 3182, www.boosyssurfschool.com. Christian Boos runs this school, offering group lessons for beginners, individual tuition or guided tours. 2-hr group lessons daily at 1100 and 1500, US$50.

Burkie's Surf School, T428 7915/230 2456, www.surfbarbados.net. Alan Burke, many times and current Barbados champion, now gives lessons to share his enthusiasm for the sport. 6 hrs group and private lessons US$195 or US$330. Board rentals US$15 per hr or US$30 per day.

Surf Barbados, T256 3906, www.surfing-barbados.com. Barry Banfield is a top surfer and offers instruction for beginners or rental boards and guided surf tours for intermediate to advanced surfers. Surf all day US$75 including instruction and board rental.

Zed's Surfing Adventures, T428 7873, www.zedsurftravel.com. Instruction for beginners; surfing tours for the more advanced. Daily 2-hr group lessons from 1000, US$80.

Tennis

Nearly all the major hotels have tennis courts and many are lit for night play.

There is a combination of public and private tennis facilities and some top class professional coaches providing tuition. The **Sir Garfield Sobers Sports Complex**, Wildey, St Michael, is the official home of the National Tennis Centre, with other main centres at Club Rockley Resort and the West Side Tennis Centre at Sunset Crest behind the Chattel House Village, Holetown. Contact Barbados Tennis Association, www.tennisbarbados.org. **A David and John Lloyd Tennis Village**, is at Sugar Hill Estate. www.sugarhillestate.com, in a development of villas and condos, with 4 floodlit courts, a central clubhouse, pool, fitness centre, restaurant and bar.

Tour operators

Adventureland, T429 3687, www.adventure landbarbados.com. Also known as Island Safari. Jeep tours of the centre of the island including Welchman Gully, Mt Hillaby and a buffet lunch on the east coast, adults US$87.50, children US$55.

Andrew Transport, T822 8007, www. andrewtransportbarbados.com. A range of tours, historical, nature, hidden villages or customized tours, 4-5 hrs, from US$50-65 including lunch and entry fees.

Sweet Barbados Island Tours Tours, T429 4327. Variety of tours: east coast, west coast, south coast, rum tours, botanic tours, history tours, prices range from US$57.50-97.50, lunch included.

Windsurfing and kitesurfing

The south coast is good for windsurfing and kitesurfing. The centre of the action for windsurfers is Silver Rock. There is a 2-mile stretch of reef providing excellent waves for wave sailors and a lagoon for those who are less confident. The best place to learn to windsurf is in the Sandy Beach area inside the lagoon, while outside the reef you can sometimes get good wave sailing. On the north coast the waves can be very big at Cow Pens and Red Backs. Access is not easy as there is only a very small each from which to launch yourself. **The International Funboard Challenge** is held in Mar. The **Barbados Windsurfing World Cup** is in Jan. The **Waterman Festival**, in Mar, is a professional international windsurfing event where you can see lots of acrobatics. There is also a competition for stand up paddling (SUP). **Last Waterman Standing** in Oct is a round-Barbados challenge for SUPers.

Kitesurfing is best done further east near the airport, at Long Beach, where the wind is side on shore. The wind is best from Nov to Jul. When the wind is light and windsurfers can't go out, then the area between Silver Sands Resort and Silver Rock Resort is good for beginners. The Casuarina Beach is also good as the wind is a bit stronger here and funnels down the coast.

Brian Talma runs **deAction Surf Shop**, Silver Sands, www.briantalma.pro. A Barbadian watersports legend, Brian was instrumental in introducing windsurfing to Barbados in the 1980s and more recently, in 2005, introduced SUPing. Here you can have instruction in surfing, windsurfing, kitesurfing and SUPing, rent or purchase boards, stay in a studio, apartment or cottage on the beach.

Contents

Footnotes

A sprint through history

1627 The first English settlers arrived to find an uninhabited island. It had been discovered earlier by the Portuguese, who named it Os Barbados, after the bearded

1639 Governor Henry Hawley founded the House of Assembly. Some 40,000 white settlers (about 1% of the population of England) arrived, mostly small farmers.

1643 Commercial production of sugar began, with plants introduced from Brazil by Dutch Jews, who also brought capital, credit, technology and markets.

1651 After the execution of King Charles I (1649), Oliver Cromwell sent a fleet to take over Royalist Barbados but his forces were held at bay for six months.

1652 The stalemate with Cromwell was resolved with the signing of the Articles of Agreement, later recognized as the Charter of Barbados by the English Parliament.

1650s Sugar revolution. Most white settlers left, plantations were now owned by a small group of whites, African slaves were brought in to work sugar plantations.

1657 Richard Ligon published 'A True and Exact History of the Island of Barbadoes… also the principal Trees and Plants There'. He described the island as "so grown with wood as there could be found no champions (fields), nor savannas for men to dwell in."

1665 Most of the forests were cleared for sugar.

1674 Richard Ford, English surveyor, drew map of Barbados showing every plantation, 800 sugar mills, water mills and cattle mills, and names of owners. By the end of the

fig trees which grew on the beaches, and left behind some wild pigs. King Charles I gave the Earl of Carlisle permission to colonize the island.

17th century there were over 400 windmills.

1686 100 prisoners deported from England to Barbados after failed Monmouth Rebellion and Judge Jeffrey's 'Bloody Assizes'.

1695-1696 Small pox epidemic.

1807 Britain abolished the African slave trade, but not slavery. Barbados exported locally bred slaves to other colonies.

1816 Easter Rebellion, slave uprising in which several hundred slaves were killed when they mistakenly thought slavery had been abolished in England. Signal stations subsequently built throughout island to give advance warning of further rebellions.

1833 Emancipation Bill passed by British parliament with slaves to undergo a period of apprenticeship. Barbadian slave owners compensated with average payments of £20 13s 8d per slave.

1838 Slavery abolished with full freedom for apprentices. However, planters carried on as before and newly freed labourers 'were given the choice of starving, working under unsatisfactory conditions, or migrating' (Barbadian historian Hilary Backles, A History of Barbados).

1840s Barbadian labourers earned half that of Trinidadians and were the lowest paid in the Caribbean (except Montserrat). Sugar prices fell with greater competition worldwide.

1843 Samuel Jackman Prescod was the first coloured member to be elected to the House of Assembly.

1850s Cholera, 29,727 died in 1854.

1890s Severe drought.

1894 Sugar exports were 50,958 tons (8837 in 1815), 97% of total exports, but market share was declining because of competition from European sugar beet, while half of all plantations were owned by absentee landlords. Capital investment and technological improvement was minimal.

1898 Hurricane devastated island.

1904-1914 About 60,000 workers went to Panama to help construct the canal, with 20,000 in 1909 alone.

1908 Yellow fever epidemic.

1919 Drought and flood.

1923 20,000 migrants left for New York.

1927 Malaria epidemic.

1930s Effects of worldwide depression felt, with unemployment, falling wages and higher imported food prices. Infant mortality was 217 per 1000 live births, compared with 58 per 1000 in Britain.

1937 Colonial authorities arrested and deported Clement Payne, a trade union organizer from Trinidad who spread word of labour unrest and riots in neighbouring islands and Marcus Garvey's teachings on pan-Africanism. Riots followed, with police shooting and killing 14, wounding 47 and arresting over 400.

1939-1945 The Second World War. Reprieve for the sugar industry with the disruption of beet growing in Europe but U-boat activity limited food imports. Rise of the trades union movement and formation of the Barbados Labour Party (BLP), headed by lawyer, Grantley Adams (1898-1971),

who had represented Clement Payne in his appeal against deportation. West India Royal Commission chaired by Lord Moyne, produced a damning report on neglect and deprivation in the British Caribbean, describing squalid and unhealthy slums and shanty towns and the dire state of education and health provision.

1940 Colonial Development and Welfare Act authorized the first funds to be spent on housing and education.

1947 The BLP won the general elections.

1950 Universal adult suffrage introduced (previously limited to property owners).

1954 Grantley Adams became the first Prime Minister of Barbados under a new system of ministerial government.

1955 Hurricane Janet caused severe destruction of infrastructure.

1956 All the British Caribbean islands agreed to create the West Indies Federation.

1958 Elections held for the West Indies Federation. Grantley Adams became Prime Minister, with headquarters in Trinidad.

1961 Jamaica withdrew from the Federation after inter-island hostility and the whole thing fell apart.

1960s Rise of tourism with introduction of long-haul jet aircraft.

1966 Barbados became independent member of the British Commonwealth. Errol Barrow of the Democratic Labour Party (DLP) was Prime Minister, 1961-1976 and since then power has alternated between the DLP and the Barbados Labour Party (BLP).

Architecture

17th century The Jacobean Drax Hall (not open to the public) and St Nicholas Abbey are two of the oldest domestic buildings in the English-speaking Americas. At this time many houses were constructed from ballast brought to the island on ships from England together with local coral stone. Many were destroyed by storms and rebuilt on the same site.

18th century The oldest ecclesiastical building dates from 1784, only because it was the only one to survive hurricanes, floods and fires. St George Parish Church was destroyed by a hurricane in 1780 and rebuilt four years later. Sugar paid for the construction of grand Georgian colonial mansions, plantation houses built of coral stone and brick ballast in the tradition of the British Empire. The British Garrison, stationed in Barbados from 1780, built hospitals, barracks and houses in the Georgian and Palladian style with grand staircases, arcades and pediments.

19th century The Victorian style can still be seen today in churches, rebuilt after hurricanes and other natural disasters, and plantation houses. Verandahs were decorated with carved wood tracery, window parapets were trimmed with filigree and sash and jalousie windows alternated on the façades in perfect proportion. Vila Nova (not open to the public) dates from this period, as do the Parliament buildings in Bridgetown. Many chattel houses mimicked the grand houses with their ornate fretwork, carved bannisters and jalousie windows in perfect proportion. Steep gable roofs were designed to withstand heavy winds and rain, fretwork provided shade and a filter against the rain, while jalousie windows, with two sets of vertical hinges and one horizontal, provided maximum protection from the sun and the wind.

20th century The last plantation house to be built was Francia (now a school), in 1910, designed by a Frenchman using a blend of French and Bajan styles with Brazilian hardwoods. With the lessening of British political and cultural influence and the rise of the USA throughout the Caribbean, more recent architecture is American in style. Office blocks of glass and steel now dwarf the houses on the outskirts of Bridgetown and many of the hotels along the south coast are concrete blocks. Innovative design has been confined to private housing, many fine examples are on show in the National Trust's Open House programme.

Index

Notes

Titles available in the Footprint *Focus* range

For the latest books, e-books and a wealth of travel information, visit us at: www.footprinttravelguides.com.

Join us on facebook for the latest travel news, product releases, offers and amazing competitions: www.facebook.com/footprintbooks.